The Road to Indianapolis

The Road to Indianapolis

Inside a Season of
Indiana High School Basketball

Mark Plaiss
and
Mike Plaiss

Bonus Books, Inc., Chicago

95 94 93 92 91   5 4 3 2 1

Library of Congress Catalog Card Number: 91-75666

International Standard Book Number: 0-929387-58-9

Bonus Books, Inc.
160 East Illinois Street
Chicago, Illinois 60611

Composition by Point West Inc., Carol Stream, IL

Printed in the United States of America

This book is dedicated to

Bud Plaiss, Robert Plaiss,
and
Bob Schuley

Contents

Acknowledgments

The authors wish to thank Jim and Pam Stevens for their help in making this book possible.

Special thanks to Mike Thomas for providing photographs.

Introduction

Not long ago a high school basketball game was played in a neighboring state. The game was between two rivals, and the small gym was packed. People were squatting in the aisles and sitting cross-legged on the floor. Brass horns and bass drums from a pep band on the stage at the far end of the gym added even more decibels to the din already rocking the rafters. Though the temperature outside hovered near zero, inside people were sweating.

Suddenly, the star of the home team, a 6-foot-7 forward, was flipped an outlet pass by a rebounding guard, and now he was streaking down the court for a breakaway bucket. No opposing player was anywhere near him, in fact, *nobody* was near him. He was all alone before the eyes of perhaps a thousand people. Dreams of glory, no doubt, danced through the young man's head.

The crowd rose in one huge swell of noise and motion. Everyone in the gym knew a slam was coming, the only question was what form would it take? Would it be a 360? Perhaps a thunderous tomahawk a la Michael Jordan? Maybe a two-handed, rim-hanging affair?

The young man rose high in the air, and as he lifted from the court, he rotated his body so that at the apex of his jump his back was to the basket. Then, in a fluid, yet powerful move, he brought the ball over his head and stuffed the ball through the hoop and nylon netting. It was a reverse slam dunk.

"Woosh!" went the crowd in unison, then it went berserk. Small children covered their ears from the noise. People jumped up and down or stamped their feet on the metal bleachers, pointing fingers and shaking fists to their young hero who trotted coolly down to the other end of the floor.

But out from underneath the basket darted the referee. In his mouth was the whistle, and his forehead and bloated cheeks were beet red. He was obviously blowing on that whistle, but because of the noise it could not be heard. His arms, though, were plainly visible, and what he was doing with his arms, and the violent manner in which he was doing it, sent the crowd into orbit.

The ref was waving off the basket. Three, four, five times he waved off the basket. The ref's eyes seemed to be focused on some faraway object. But by this time he was nearly at center court, and coming to a halt he calmly gave the call—walking.

"Boo!" thundered the crowd. Jeers and catcalls rained down upon the ref. But as the ire of the crowd followed the ref as he hustled downcourt, curious things began to be said among the fans themselves. Yes, the player took steps, they admitted, but so what? His move to the basket was fabulous, they asserted, so how could the points not be allowed? Besides, the pros do such things all the time, they cried, why not our guy?

Here was a group of basketball fans admitting the player had committed an illegal move, but who believed the infraction should be overlooked due to the degree of difficulty of the slam dunk. What was important to these fans was the show, not the game. They wanted a slam dunk contest, not a basketball game. The rules were subordinate to flashy moves. It never seemed to occur to them that the reason their hero was able to make such a move was because he took two and a half steps too many.

High school may be the last bastion of pure basketball. The pro game often resembles big-time wrestling, especially beneath the boards, and the collegiates seem determined to be the pro's wannabes. Preps, though, still play the game more within the rules, more within the boundaries it was intended to be played, the above illustration notwithstanding. The reason for this may be the teen-agers' lack of maturity, lack of sophistication, and perhaps more importantly, lack of money. Many states produce outstanding high school basketball players, Illinois, California, and New York come quickly to mind. But nowhere is high school basketball more popular, more closely analyzed, more argued over than in Indiana.

"High school sports brings a community together," says Charlie Jenkins, a veteran high school sports announcer for WXVW radio in Jeffersonville. "In Ohio or Pennsylvania it might be high school football or wrestling. But in Indiana it is definitely high school basketball. Almost any community you go to has a radio station, and 99 percent of them broadcast high school basketball." And the Hoosier state has produced some greats of the game as well. Does Oscar Robertson or Larry Bird or John Wooden ring a bell?

Cruise along Interstate 70 until you reach the exit for New Castle. Zip north on Indiana Highway 3 for about four miles until you reach Trojan Lane. Hang a right. There, at the crest of a knoll, you will find a multi-million dollar shrine—the Indiana Basketball Hall of Fame Museum. Just in case you get lost, it is located a stone's throw from New Castle High School—home of the largest high school gymnasium in the world. It seats over 9,000 fans. It's a pit—literally. The floor of the gym is sunk below ground level with the top row of bleachers being on the ground level as you walk into the gymnasium. When over 9,000 crazies start stomping their feet, clapping their hands, whistling, and screaming, the visiting team only wishes it could crawl out of that blasted pit.

Moved to New Castle in the early summer of 1990 from its antiquated quarters in Indianapolis, the Hall of Fame Museum houses the history of Indiana basketball. Although dedicated to basketball at all levels—prep through professional—the emphasis is on high school basketball.

Inside the 14,000-square-foot brick and glass museum you see ancient laced basketballs and quaint scoreboards, fading photographs of past glory, lettermen's sweaters, megaphones, mascots, melted-down rims, yellowed newspaper clippings, scorebooks from championship games, trophies, jerseys, shoes, and pennants. You can watch a film on the history of the game in the sixty-seat Marsh Theater or push a button and see a videotape of the 1982 double-overtime state finals victory of Plymouth over Gary Roosevelt. From the iron rafters high overhead hang banners proclaiming sectional, regional, semi-state, or state victories. Some banners are from schools long gone, lost to the consolidation frenzy of the fifties and early sixties; schools with names that wax poetic—Birdseye, Ireland, Ferdinand, Holland, Otwell.

Outside the museum, carved in the center of the courtyard, is a map of the state, seventy feet long and thirty-six feet wide, composed from thousand of bricks. Inscribed on most of the bricks, at a donation fee of at least $100, are names or events that make up the mosaic of Indiana high school basketball. Near the center of the state, for example, is a brick carved merely with the name "Oscar Robertson." Down at the bottom of the state a brick is chiseled "Wheatland Jeeps Class of 1939." Up and over a little bit is another brick that reads, "Bobby Plump, Milan, 1954."

Milan. Does any other single word mean so much to Indiana basketball? When Bobby Plump from tiny Milan buried the field goal to defeat perennial powerhouse Muncie Central back in 1954, could he have imagined that thirty-two years later Hollywood would be inspired by his team's efforts to make a film called *Hoosiers*? Every year kids in small schools from Henryville to Hebron look to the Miracle of Milan for inspiration and hope. Coaches have even been known to show *Hoosiers* to their teams prior to tournament games. Milan is not simply the name of a particular school that happened to win the state championship one year. It can be persuasively argued that Milan is the reason Indiana retains a single-class system and tournament for basketball. Without Milan Indiana would probably have conformed to the national norm of a multiclass system and tournament years ago. Milan, then, is a dream, an ideal on which Indiana has banked its basketball hopes, success, and future.

Indiana stretches north from the knobs on the Ohio River, through the central fertile flatlands, to the sandy shores of Lake Michigan. It is the smallest state west of the Alleghenies, except for Hawaii. Indiana is corn, hogs, steel, and racing. Unlike its larger neighbors, Indiana has never had professional sports franchises the whole state could identify with, and besides, professional teams were so close at hand. Chicago had the White Sox, Cubs, and Bears; Detroit the Lions and Tigers; Cincinnati had the Reds. St. Louis even pulled some Hoosier backers. Indianapolis now has the Pacers and Colts, but these are relatively new franchises that have yet to gain statewide support.

What all Hoosiers could rally around, though, was their local basketball team. While the Buckeye rooted for the Reds or the Indians or the Browns, the Hoosier pulled for the Jeeps, Spuds, or Slicers.

Rivalries were as intense as any in the pro games. When Huntingburg–Jasper, New Albany–Jeffersonville, Anderson–Marion, LaCrosse–Kouts, or East Chicago Washington–East Chicago Roosevelt took the floor, tension and tempers ran high. So did the attendance.

In 1990, California, the most populous state in the nation, drew 20,000 people to its final two-day tournament. That same year Indiana, ranked fourteenth in population, drew over 40,000 to its championship game alone. Of course, attendance was helped along by the game being played in a domed stadium. That's right, a high school basketball game in a *domed stadium*. The Final Four was played at the Hoosier Dome, and attendance for the entire four-week tournament nearly tipped the million mark. And attendance could have been higher than it was had the entire seating capacity of the dome been utilized. The dome was partitioned, though, and approximately 20,000 seats remained empty. Officials agree the seats could have been sold.

Sectionals, regionals, semistate, state—from childhood the Hoosier knows this litany of tournament progression. The sectionals are played more or less at the county or bi-county level, usually pitting rivals against one another who have already met during the regular season. The sectionals, usually played in the area's largest gym, can span as many as five days or as few as two, depending on the size of the sectional. The Fort Wayne sectional, for example, starts on Tuesday and ends Saturday night. The Jeffersonville sectional, on the other hand, begins Friday and ends Saturday. Thereafter, the regionals, semistate, and state rounds are each played on one day, with four teams coming into each site. The winners of the morning game advance to play in the evening game to determine the champion.

The regionals are at sixteen sites throughout the state, edging ever closer to Indianapolis. The Sweet Sixteen is played at four semistate locations: Roberts Arena in Evansville (or Indiana State in Terre Haute), Hinkle Fieldhouse in Indianapolis, Mackey Arena at Purdue in West Lafayette, and The Coliseum in Fort Wayne (or Joyce Arena at Notre Dame in South Bend). The Final Four is in Indianapolis at the Hoosier Dome.

When the show finally hits the dome, it resembles any NCAA Regional basketball game. Hundreds of reporters line press row. Radio station banners in every hue and shape drape over a myriad of tables. Television cameras and cables litter every nook and cranny surrounding the floor. And when you look up into the stands you don't see a seat. For over a half century the state finals have been sold-out. Only when the Final Four was moved from Market Square Arena to the dome in 1990 did tickets go on sale for the general public. Prior to that, tickets were sold only to the participating schools. It's hard to believe all of this fuss is for the sake of watching teen-agers play basketball.

What follows is a look at one season of Indiana high school basketball as it marches through its regular season, races through its tournament, and crowns its single champion. When one mentions Indiana high school basketball one usually thinks of past glories, the sectionals won, the regionals lost, the what-might-have-beens, the thirty-foot desperation shots to beat the buzzer and immortality. Decades following a game, men and women will sit in basements or in dens or in kitchens or living rooms and explain to their children how their team lost that regional by just one point by some kid who hit a last-second basket while sitting on his butt near the free-throw line. Such things are just not forgotten. Rarely, though, does one think of the now.

This book is about the making of the now.

Regular Season

Preseason Buildup

A collective sigh of relief was heard among basketball coaches at the beginning of the 1990–91 season. Damon Bailey, the baby-faced terror from Bedford North Lawrence who guided the Stars to the 1990 state championship and who finished with a record 3,134 career points, finally moved onto (surprise) Bloomington and Bob Knight's Hoosiers.

That sigh masked a "good riddance" among the coaches in the Hoosier Hills Conference, the conference that includes Bedford North Lawrence. No longer would they have to rack their brains trying to figure out ways to stop the all-time-career-scoring-leader-Mr. Basketball-Trester-Award-winning-IU-bound Bailey.

When the preseason Associated Press poll appeared on November 13, the ranking showed a balance of strength throughout the state from north to south. On top was Gary Roosevelt. Martinsville and Evansville Bosse, from central and southern Indiana, fell into the second and third spots, respectively. Indianapolis Pike and Vincennes, again from southern Indiana, rounded out the fourth and fifth positions.

Gary Roosevelt, beaten by Anderson in the Lafayette semistate the previous year, returned one of the premier big men in the country, Glenn Robinson. The 6-foot-9, 205 pound Robinson, highly touted for

Mr. Basketball and ranked one of the top twenty players in the country in *Street & Smith's College/Prep Basketball*, averaged 21.5 ppg, 10 boards per game, and 4.5 blocked shots per game as a junior in the 1989–90 season. Deadly around the basket, Robinson could spin and drive to the hole in the blink of an eye and with the force of a train. Roosevelt coach Ron Heflin called Robinson the "best player in the state," and the cutthroat recruiting of Robinson by such schools as Purdue, Indiana, and Illinois seemed to justify Heflin's boast.

But Roosevelt was not a one-person team; two other starters returned from the 1989–90 team that finished 23–3. Six-foot-five senior Carlos Floyd (7 ppg, 5 rpg) and 6-foot-3 Ryan Harding (9 ppg) joined Robinson to round out the frontcourt. The question mark was the backcourt and a weak bench. Not helping matters any was the loss of George Butler. The 6-foot-2 Butler was a junior and a starter on the 1989–90 team. But he turned nineteen during the summer and was declared ineligible to play another year. Butler had lost a year of school as fourth grader due to heart problems.

Robinson, though, was not the only hotshot in the state. Alan Henderson was another Mr. Basketball candidate and another top twenty pick in *Street & Smith's*. The 6-foot-9, 200 pound senior from unranked Brebeuf High School, a Jesuit-run school on the north side of Indianapolis, was just as at home as an outside shooter as Robinson was at home down close. In his junior year Henderson averaged 29.7 ppg, and 14.2 rebounds. In addition, he shot 55 percent from the field (Robinson averaged 65 percent) and averaged two assists per game. Henderson also had an eye for the three-pointer and was known to block as many as ten shots in one game. Like Robinson, Henderson experienced fierce recruiting. But unlike Robinson, Henderson was joined by only one other starter from the previous year's 16–5 team.

Although Robinson and Henderson were the top two contenders for Mr. Basketball as the season prepared to open, other players throughout the state were making noise, too. Just down the road from Mr. Robinson's neighborhood, for example, was Brandon Brantley at Andrean. The 6-foot-8 senior was one of three starters returning from the 18–5 Hammond sectional champion team. Brantley and Robinson would meet in their team's season opener at Andrean.

A little farther east at Michigan City Elston junior Charles Macon was already catching the attention of major universities. The 6-foot-7 center averaged 20 ppg and 10 rpg in the 1989–90 season and was the linchpin of four other returning starters.

What do you do when you have a front line that averages 6-foot-6, a guard who can pop threes, manage to win twenty-four games, but still you come up short? If you are coach Joe Mullan of Evansville Bosse you plan some revenge over a long, long off-season. Knocked off by Damon Bailey and company in the 1989–90 semistate by just one point, Mullan and his Bulldogs were ready to play. "We'll be among the best in the state," Mullan said matter-of-factly. Leading the charge would be three veterans. Six-foot-seven senior Andy Elkins (19.2 ppg, 11 rpg) and 6-foot-4 senior Ron Darrett (19 ppg, 7 rpg) returned from the front line. Six-foot Antwan Pope returned as guard.

What about the small schools? Well, Kouts (town population, 1,619) was looking to rebound from a respectable 13–9 record and a tie for fourth in the Porter County Conference with Sam Obermeyer (17.1 ppg, 9 rpg), Brad Redelman (14.9 ppg), and Greg Larson (14.9 ppg). The *Vidette-Messenger* of Valparaiso predicted the Mustangs to win the conference.

At Charlestown, town population of 5,596, 6-foot-9 senior forward Chad Gilbert returned from a 21–3 team that won the 1990 Floyd Central sectional. Though the Pirates lost five of their top six players, the 18–2 junior varsity team gave reason for hope of another sectional and Mid-Southern Conference title.

Every basketball season, it seems, brings yet another cry for class ball. The 1990–91 season was no different. This time the crusade was led by Marty Gohmann of New Albany.

Gohmann was the chairman of something called the Committee for Small School Basketball, and it was his hope to give the little guys some hope, hope as far as the semistate round anyway.

Gohmann's idea was to have a separate tourney for the small schools as far as the semistate round. Then, the winner of the small school semistate would play the winner of the "big" school semistate, guaranteeing a small school would always be in at least a semistate championship game.

The Associated Press reported that at the October 31 meeting of the Indiana High School Athletic Association (IHSAA) executive meeting, commissioner Gene Cato brought up the "two-in-one" class tournament alignment, but emphasized that it was only a hearing on the matter. In fact, Cato emphasized he did not endorse the idea.

"In my position, I hear a lot of complaints and concern," Cato told the Associated Press. "But Indiana is one of three states that does not have class basketball. I hope we never see more than one state tourney. Last year, I don't believe any other state with a class system could attract 41,000-plus the way we did at the Hoosier Dome.''

The IHSAA executive committee was to have made its recommendations in April or May of 1991.

The sun shined on October 15, 1990, the temperature reaching the low sixties. High, white clouds streaked across a blue, autumn sky.

Much of the scuttlebutt that day centered around Soviet President Mikhail Gorbachev receiving the Nobel Peace Prize and Israel stating it would not cooperate with a United Nations inquiry into the killings on the Temple Mount.

On a lighter note, Oakland's Dave Stewart and Cincinnati's Jose Rijo were about to open the World Series at Riverfront Stadium. The University of Virginia was the No. 1 college football team in the country.

It was also the first day of high school basketball practice in the Hoosier State.

At the corner of Harrison and Twenty-fifth Avenue in Gary, inside the John D. Smith Athletic Complex of Roosevelt High School, were fourteen young men. They sat cross-legged at midcourt in the Bo Mallard Gymnasium. Before them stood their coach, Ron Heflin.

''If you stay focused on our goal, and if you match up to the potential I know you have, there is nothing you cannot do. You will win,'' said Heflin. ''The goal of this team is to win our conference and to improve upon last year's record (23–3), to get back to Indianapolis. But you must focus, and not get distracted.''

High above them, hanging on the walls, was a large, gold banner bordered in black. ''Gary Roosevelt State Champions 1968,'' was printed in large, black letters. Ryan Harding, one of the players sitting at Heflin's feet, glanced up at it.

Heflin, dressed in a white cotton golf shirt and black pants, looked down into the eyes of the players who followed his every move. It was hard to hear what he was saying, for the cheerleaders were nearby practicing their routines. Then Heflin clapped his hands and yelled, ''Let's go!'' and the players jumped up itching to get their hands on a basketball.

Ron Heflin, fifty-two, was beginning his sixteenth season at Gary Roosevelt. Twice in that period he had led a team to the Final Four in Indianapolis. In 1982, his first trip, he made it to the championship game by beating previously undefeated Evansville Bosse 58–57 in the morning game. But that night Plymouth, led by Scott Skiles, nipped the Panthers 75–74 in double overtime. Heflin took another team to Indianapolis in 1987, but couldn't get past the morning game. Roosevelt fell to Richmond 66–60.

Heflin, standing with his arms crossed, watched the young men rise from the floor. Heflin is not an emotional man. He doesn't appear comfortable in crowds. After big wins he quickly retires to the locker room, allowing his players and assistant coaches the glory. He does not stalk the sidelines during a game scowling or pleading with refs; he does not berate or plead with his players. Usually, he leans back in his chair, his hands clasping one knee, closely watching the action on the floor. When something does catch his eye, he stands up, and with his hands over his head, gets the players to do what he wants them to do.

But he doesn't take any crap from his players, either. He is a disciplinarian both on and off the court. When Glenn Robinson, undoubtedly the star of this team, loafs or does not apply himself in school, Heflin comes down on him. Hard. The other players see that and appreciate Heflin's fairness; they know he will discipline the star of the team as well as the journeymen.

Heflin also demands discipline on the playing floor. He knows this team likes to run, to play, as he says, "An up-tempo game." That's fine with him. In fact, with this particular team, he prefers it, because they have the talent to do it, and he feels they can do it better than anyone around. But he will not tolerate a *ragged* up-tempo game. It must be controlled, and they better damn well get back on defense. "We will not be a team that just plays run-down-the-floor-and-shoot," Heflin says.

Heflin is a tall man, about 6-foot-4 or so. He played basketball at Roosevelt in the late fifties under Louis "Bo" Mallard and went on to play more basketball at Tennessee State.

One of the players that stood up from sitting on the floor rose higher than the others, and while all the other players wore brown, perforated jerseys bearing "Velt" on the front, this young man wore a plain gold jersey. His name was Glenn Robinson.

The 6-foot-9, 210-pound Robinson was beginning his final season at Roosevelt knowing that he was the center, in more ways than one, of his team. It was he who would carry the high expectations of coaches, alumni, and fans, not to mention teammates, on his shoulders. Roosevelt had come close last year, reaching the semifinals. This year he knew people were expecting more. One of those people was himself.

Robinson was a lot like his coach—quiet, expressionless, content to let his work on the floor speak for itself. He was not noted for pumping his fist in the air after hitting one of his seemingly effortless turnaround jumpers or after he wowed the crowd with a monster jam. He just did his work, then headed off downcourt. He and Carlos Floyd and Ryan Harding had played together since grade school. They had dreamed the same dreams, but more importantly they knew one another. Knew how one another played, knew one another's weaknesses, knew one another's strengths. They were seniors now, and this was their last chance.

He was not noted for his academic work, either, which is unfair, because until a year ago his grades were fine.

''Glenn was fine academically,'' Heflin said, ''until late last year. His grades began falling then. And that was because of too much emphasis on basketball. He was spreading himself too thin. He was playing on two AAU teams and was readying himself for an exhibition game against the Russians. He didn't miss any school, but when he did try to study, he was too tired. He's got the head for it, he just needs to apply it to books as well as ball.''

Robinson knows that he will have to apply himself academically if he wants to play for the schools that have come courting him. High on his list are Purdue, Illinois, and Michigan. He expects to make a decision soon about which college he will attend, and he hopes the SAT classes he attends every morning from 7:30 to 8:30 will help him.

Their itchy hands couldn't get ahold of a basketball; Heflin wouldn't let them touch one. Instead, they practiced guarding one another. Heflin split the team in half and had them move the length of the court, one person guarding another.

''Defense is with the feet!'' Heflin yelled. ''Move your feet!''

Next he had them all run sideways around the perimeter of the court, putting one leg in front, then the other. Then it was back to more defensive drills.

"Eighty percent of what I do in practice concerns defense," Heflin said, "'cause defense wins games. I can have Glenn put 50 points on the board, but if he allows 50 from the other team, what good is his?"

Heflin showed them where to stand when defending someone, what to do with their arms, what to watch for, how to keep their feet sliding.

Then it was over. They had practiced without touching a basketball. Twenty-nine days remained until their first game; one hundred and fifty nine until the state finals.

If they made it that far.

2

Early Season Matchups

Oregon-Davis at Kouts
Saturday, November 17, 1990

While Lori Johnson nervously sang the national anthem a cappella on the stage at the far end of the court, the crowd of about 400 fans stood in rapt attention. During the breaks in the song when Lori took deep, shaky breaths, there was only silence. No one coughed, no one sniffed a snotty nose, no baby cried, no one whispered to his neighbor, no one giggled. In fact no one even sang along. All eyes were focused on the flag hanging above midcourt.

Welcome to game night at Kouts High School.

Located about ten miles south of Valparaiso in rural southern Porter County just a couple of blocks east of Highway 49, Kouts has a student enrollment of fewer than 300 and is a member of the Porter County Conference. Kouts is also touted by the local press to win the conference.

Marty Gaff, entering his eighth year as head coach of the Mustangs, has six lettermen returning from the previous year's 13–9 squad that finished in a three-way tie for fourth place in the conference.

Gaff's big men are 6-foot-7 seniors Sam Obermeyer and Brad Redelman. Joining them on the front line is a junior, 6-foot-4 Tom McNeil. Seniors Greg Larson and David Hamstra fill in the backcourt of this nine-man team.

The Mustangs' opponent this Saturday night, the opening night for both teams, is Oregon-Davis, a consolidation of Grovertown and Hamlet High Schools from neighboring Starke County. The Bobcats have fallen on hard times. The 1989–90 team finished a dismal 2–17, and only one experienced player returned from that squad to a 1990–91 team that doesn't hold much promise. But oh that 1987–88 season.

The film *Hoosiers* had recently been released that season. The Bobcats had raced through the regular season with twenty victories against only one defeat, and the air was filled with comparisons between Oregon-Davis, student population 350, nestled in tiny Hamlet, and the mythic Hickory High of *Hoosiers*. The Bobcats soon caught the eye of *USA Today*, and when the Bobcats traveled down Highway 10 to play the championship game of the North Judson sectional, a sectional it had never won, the team bus was followed by a train of Bobcat supporters. Car after car blared its horn and flew red, black, and white streamers from its radio antennas and bumpers. And when Oregon-Davis, or simply O-D as those fans say, beat LaCrosse for their first sectional title, none other than the *New York Times* and ABC-TV were there to witness the event. Dan Warkentien, then head coach at O-D and now at Lebanon, even appeared on ABC's "Nightline."

But all of that is ancient history now. The two teams take the floor to open their 1990–91 seasons, and within minutes Kouts has the game under control. O-D forward Matt Shively hits a jumper at the 5:37 mark of the first quarter to bring the Bobcats to within one point of Kouts, 7–6, but that is as close as O-D will come the rest of the game. The Mustangs then race out on a 22–11 run sparked by Obermeyer's 12 points, Larson's 7, and Redelman's 6 to put Kouts up 30–17 at the end of the first quarter. A frustrated O-D fan, no doubt awash with memories of the Bobcat's glory year, is momentarily heartened, though. O-D guard Brad Yung snares a Kouts air ball and races down the court for an uncontested layup. "That's it, that's it," cries the fan in encouragement, "you got it, right, keep going, keep. . . oh no, you big dummy!" groans the fan as the layup ricochets off the backboard.

When the rout ends an hour and a half later, Kouts has given notice it intends to take no prisoners this season. Obermeyer and Larson each finish with 24 points, with Obermeyer grabbing 17 rebounds. Redelman chipped in another 12 points. The team nailed 5 three-pointers. The final score is 91–48.

''It's always nice to win your opener,'' says a matter-of-fact Gaff outside his team's locker room after the game. His tie is loosened and the collar is unbuttoned. He leans up against the wall with his hands in his pockets.

''We moved the ball well, and we did what we wanted to do which was to run and force them into an up-tempo game. But I thought our defense was nonexistent. We allowed them the ball inside far too much, and our guards were just standing around. We also turned the ball over too many times. We need to work on our ball handling.''

But what about Obermeyer and Larson?

''Those two are gonna have good nights,'' says Gaff. ''They can shoot. And they're gonna have to have a lot of good nights if we expect to win some games this year.''

Gary Roosevelt at Andrean
Thursday, November 19, 1990

A standing-room-only crowd of 1,800 packed the gym at Andrean High School to witness the season opener for both No. 1-ranked Roosevelt and No. 14-ranked Andrean. But they also came to witness the matchup between 6-foot-9 Glenn Robinson and 6-foot-8 Brandon Brantley. For Purdue fans, the game was a foreshadower of things to come.

Back on November 1, in a press conference held at Roosevelt's gym, Robinson announced he would attend Purdue the following year. The choice was really no surprise, for Robinson had hinted strongly for the past several weeks that Purdue was his choice.

Robinson had intended to wait until the April signing, but he was constantly being hounded by college coaches, so he decided on the early signing to keep the hounds at bay.

''Every night I was interrupted from doing my homework by the phone,'' said Robinson. ''Seven or eight times a night.''

Coach Heflin was feeling the heat, too. ''My practices were being interrupted three or four times each day.''

Purdue came knocking early, in Robinson's sophomore year, and it paid off. "I feel comfortable with the team," Robinson said.

Brantley had signed earlier in the year.

The fans were not disappointed. Roosevelt's 66–60 overtime victory showed that Roosevelt was mortal, but that Robinson intended to exert his influence in what he considered his neighborhood.

Early on it appeared Roosevelt could do no wrong. The Panther's full-court press forced Andrean into 7 first-quarter turnovers, and Roosevelt zoomed out to a 14–9 first-quarter lead.

But Andrean settled down in the second period, committing only two turnovers in the quarter. Robinson and Brantley were nearly even at the half. Brantley scored 15 of Andrean's 25 first-half points, while Robinson netted 16 of Roosevelt's 31.

In the third quarter Roosevelt enjoyed their biggest lead of the ball game going up 39–27 at the 6:35 mark. But Andrean went on an 8–0 run, sparked by Brantley's 6, to cut the lead to 39–35.

The game shouldn't have gone into overtime at all. With twenty-four seconds remaining in regulation Ryan Harding went to the free-throw line to shoot two. He hit the first to stretch the Roosevelt lead to 55–52, but he missed the second.

On Andrean's ensuing possession Chris Artis nailed a three-pointer from the top of the key with four seconds left to send the game into overtime and the Andrean fans into orbit. But Roosevelt really had no one to blame but themselves. Twice in the fourth quarter they missed the front ends of one-and-one foul shots. For the entire game they were 18 of 30 from the free-throw line.

Roosevelt got a break when at the 1:44 mark of the overtime period Brantley fouled out.

Roosevelt's free-throw shooting woes continued in the overtime period. Leading by four, 61–57 with just 1:10 left in overtime, Roosevelt's Rickie Wedlow went to the line for a one-and-bonus. Sink both and Roosevelt's up six, probably out of reach with so little time left. Hit one, and they're still up five. You guessed it, he missed the front end.

Andrean rebounded and with exactly a minute left Chris Artis connected on a driving shot to cut it to 61–59.

Then with forty-nine seconds remaining Roosevelt's Ryan Harding was fouled and sent to the line. Harding, who hit only 3 of 14 from the field, stepped to the line with the entire 1,800 fans screaming their heads off. He hit the first to the "woosh" of the Roosevelt fans to push the score out to 62–59. Again he took the ball from the ref, dribbled, and fired. Swish. 63–59, Roosevelt.

The Panthers needed the cushion, for with thirty-five seconds left Roosevelt's Darryl Woods fouled Rob Lemmons. Lemmons stepped to the line for the one-and-bonus. Again the crowd screamed, and Lemmons sank the first. He missed the second, and Andrean was stuck at 60. That was the last point they would score.

With nineteen seconds remaining Darryl Woods went to the free-throw line for a one-and-one. He hit the first, but missed the second, making it 64–60. And with time expiring Robinson ended the game on an exclamation point by slamming home the final two points. Roosevelt 66, Andrean 60.

Robinson led Roosevelt with 24 points, 13 rebounds, and 2 blocked shots. Four of the baskets were monstrous slams. But Robinson scored only 8 points in the second half.

Brantley, on the other hand, led all scorers with 27 points and 16 rebounds.

"We should never have been in overtime," coach Heflin said. "We had them by 12, but we couldn't hit our free throws. I thought our defense shut down Lemmons (7 points) and Lustina (9), and that was our game plan."

Heflin was also concerned with Robinson's play in the second half.

"Glenn's gonna be double- and triple-teamed all year," Heflin said, "but he has to take it. He's gonna get beat on and pounded on, but he's gotta expect it and play on."

Andrean coach Bob Buscher said, "We played them hard. They're the No. 1 team in the state, and we almost beat them. But Roosevelt's awfully tough."

Bedford at Bloomington North
Saturday, November 24, 1990

Bedford North Lawrence was without Damon Bailey for the first time in four years. How would they function without him?

Before Bedford played a single game the Associated Press ranked the Stars fifteenth in the state. Despite losing Mr. Basketball, Bedford returned five players from the 29–2 state championship team.

Six-foot-two senior Jason Lambrecht, 6-foot-2 Johnny Mike Gilbert, and 6-foot Chad Mills filled up the frontcourt, while Alan Bush, the coach's son, hoped to add some points from the perimeter.

In their opening game the Stars routed Salem 67–50. But that was on their home court. The real test was a game on the road against some stiff competition. That was Bloomington North.

The Cougars of Bloomington North were unrated in the preseason poll, but they possessed a threat in 5-foot-10 senior point guard Derrick Cross who averaged 15.4 ppg in his junior year. Dangerous from outside, Cross also had the quickness to penetrate. And he didn't leave it all at the offensive end; he played tight defense, too.

The Stars arrived in Bloomington accompanied by a busload of Bedford Boosters. These fans were mostly middle-aged men and women clad in red sweaters who nearly outnumbered the hometown crowd.

The Stars quickly gave the red-sweater set something to cheer about. Bush and Landon Graves each drilled three-pointers to help Bedford pull away to a quick 10–6 lead. But then the Stars went cold, and for nearly the last four minutes of the first quarter, the Stars failed to score a point. The Cougars then went on an 8–0 run, led by forward James Warfield's 6 points.

In the second period Bloomington pulled away from Bedford, going up by ten at the 5:09 mark when Cross drilled a three from the top of the key to make the score 23–13.

Bloomington then became generous by allowing the Stars to score seven straight points at the free-throw line to pull within 25–20 with 2:20 left in the first half.

The teams then traded baskets with Bloomington's Tony Bodie adding two free throws with ten seconds left to end the first half with the Cougars on top 33–26.

But Bedford exploded in the third quarter. The Stars raced out to a 7–4 run to pull within 37–33 before the Cougars called time-out with 3:27 remaining in the period. But the time-out was not helpful for Bloomington. The Stars went on a 12–0 run and forced Bloomington into 5 turnovers. Mills scored a total of 7 third-period points with Bush and Lambrecht each scoring 4. The period ended 45–37 with Bedford on top. They never relinquished the lead. Cross hit 3 three-pointers for the Cougars in the final period, but it wasn't enough. The final was 70–61. Cross led all scorers with 22 points.

''At the half I told them we were not attacking the basket, that we were playing tentative,'' said Bedford coach Dan Bush. ''We were spending too much time dribbling from side to side, instead of trying to attack the basket. Even early in the third we were doing that, but our defense got us going in the third. We forced some turnovers and we finally got some rebounds. Chad [Mills] was more aggressive in the second half and that helped a lot. We couldn't contain Cross in the fourth, but what are you going to do? He's going to get his points.''

And who leads this team now that Damon is gone?

''Lambrecht and Mills have been through all this before,'' said Bush. ''The other guys look to them for leadership. Those two are gonna have to take control.''

Valparaiso at Roosevelt
Friday, November 30, 1990

It was finally time to go home. After playing three games on the road, one of which—Andrean—had proved difficult, Gary Roosevelt was finally going to play their home opener. Valparaiso was to be the victim.

The Vikings were 1–1 and young. Roosevelt, of course, had Purdue-bound, 6-foot-9, 210-pound Glenn Robinson. But the Panthers also had senior forwards 6-foot-5 Carlos Floyd, and 6-foot-2 Ryan Harding. The game didn't promise to be much of one, and it wasn't.

Roosevelt rushed out to a 6–0 lead in the first 1:53 of the game. And just as soon as Valparaiso's Gabe Wright hit a 15 footer to pull the Vikings back to within 6–4 at the 5:00 mark, the Panthers went on an 11–0 run to end the quarter with a 17–4 lead. Not helping the Vikings any was the Roosevelt defense that allowed the Vikings only 2 of 11 shooting and forced 9 turnovers.

The Viking's disaster continued into the middle of the second quarter. Then, with Roosevelt leading 23–6, Valparaiso got hot and went on a 10–0 binge, fueled by Eric Utterback's 6 points. With 2:47 remaining in the half Valparaiso had made it a respectable 23–16.

But Robinson hit both ends of a one-and-one and Rickie Wedlow drilled a jumper from the right side to keep the Vikings at arm's length 27–16. In the final 2:33 of the half the teams basically just traded baskets allowing the Panthers to take a 32–22 lead to the locker room.

Roosevelt's Jeffrey Graham, who was scoreless in the first half, caught fire in the third, scoring 10 points in the period on five of eight shooting from the field. The Panthers methodically built a seventeen-point lead, 48–31, with 4:37 remaining in the period before Valpo called time-out. Graham hit two field goals while Robinson slammed a couple home and connected on a couple more free throws during that period.

After the time-out, and for the next three minutes, Roosevelt hit only one field goal, a jumper by Graham. The other seven points came from the free-throw line to give the Panthers a 57–38 lead when Valpo again called time-out with 1:17 remaining in the third quarter.

When play resumed, Roosevelt guard Darryl Woods stole the ball from Valpo's Gabe Wright and flipped an outlet pass to Robinson who slammed home a two-handed monster, only for the ref to wave it off. Woods had walked giving the pass to Robinson. But the Panthers fired in another three points before the quarter ended to take a 61–43 lead into the final period.

Roosevelt opened the fourth with a 9–0 run, including a layup and a three-pointer by Graham that started the run, and some of the Valpo fans began heading for the door. That was probably a smart move, for the Panthers went on to outscore Valpo 28–12 in that quarter to post an 89–55 win.

Robinson finished with 26 points, 14 rebounds, and 2 blocked shots. Also hitting above 20 points was Jeffrey Graham with 22. Two other Panthers scored in double figures, Carlos Floyd with 13 and Darryl Woods with 11.

Valparaiso's only player in double figures was Gabe Wright with 10.

"Valpo is a very inexperienced team, but they're gonna get better," coach Heflin said outside the locker room. "Graham can shoot the ball, that's true. He had the shots in the first half, but they just wouldn't fall. Valpo was sagging in on Glenn, and I expected that, but still he got his points. However, I was not pleased with the way we moved the ball. Not at all. We allowed them to set the tempo of the game. They wanted to slow it down, and that's not the way we play. It destroyed our timing, and I believe that's why they were successful in the second period."

3

December Shootouts

St. Louis
Thursday, December 6, 1990

"Hey, I went to see Gary Roosevelt play last night."

"Another winner?"

"They're 5–0 now."

"Great! Where'd they play?"

"St. Louis."

St. Louis? Missouri? And on a Thursday even, a school night? Well, yes.

Twelve teams, one as far away as Columbia, South Carolina, gathered at Kiel Auditorium in downtown St. Louis on December 6 to play a little ball, like from 11:00 A.M. until 11:00 P.M. A basketball junkie's dream fix. From Indiana came Gary Roosevelt and Evansville Bosse.

They came to play at the Coca-Cola/KMOX Shootout; once a gathering of just local teams, it has now expanded to bring in some of the top talent in the country. It was the tenth anniversary of the Shootout, and much of the buzz in the air centered around the center from Gary—Glenn Robinson. Many wanted to see if he was as tough as the press clips said he was.

And the Shootout had seen some tough players in its ten-year run. Players like Danny Ferry, now with the Cleveland Cavaliers, Alonzo Mourning, who plays for Georgetown, LaPhonso Ellis, now with Notre Dame, and Jerrod Mustaf, who played college ball at Maryland then on to the NBA with the New York Knicks. In five of the past seven years the nation's top-ranked high school player had participated in the Shootout. And while this year's marquee game didn't compare to the hoopla surrounding the matchup between LaPhonso Ellis and Alonzo Mourning back in 1987, it did pack 'em in tight.

The Gary game was scheduled for 8:00 P.M., and their opponent was the Kahoks of Collinsville High School from Collinsville, Illinois, the No. 1-ranked team in the St. Louis area.

Why St. Louis, coach Heflin?

"Well, it's a prestigious event," Heflin said, "and besides, we'll take the kids on some educational tours of the city, it'll be a good trip."

The Panthers flew in Wednesday evening and stayed at the Marriott Pavilion, the headquarters of all the teams playing in the Shootout. The Marriott is within walking distance of Kiel Auditorium.

Heflin put his team through an early Thursday morning workout before going off to see such sights as St. Louis University. Then it was back to the hotel for rest.

Collinsville matched up well with Gary, their front line consisting of 6-foot-7 center Kyle Jones, 6-foot-5 forward-guard Richard Keene, and 6-foot-6 forward Mike Chaney. Keene, a junior who has started on the varsity since his freshman year, averaged 21 ppg during his sophomore year. Jones averaged 13 ppg.

But after just one quarter of play, Roosevelt was clearly in control of the game. Three seconds after Glenn Robinson knocked the opening tip to Ryan Harding, Harding buried a jumper from the right corner. It was all downhill for Collinsville from that point until late in the fourth quarter when the Kahoks rallied. At the end of the first period the Panthers led by 10, thanks to Harding's 8 (including 2 three-pointers) and Carlos Floyd's 6 (4 from the free-throw line). At halftime Roosevelt's lead was 18, the Panthers' defense allowing only 5 Collinsville points in the second period.

The third period began with a 10–0 Collinsville run, spurred by back-to-back three-pointers by Keene to open the quarter. Roosevelt called time-out with 5:50, and that cooled off the Kahoks. When play resumed Robinson wowed the crowd with a tomahawk slam.

Roosevelt allowed only two Collinsville points for the remainder of the period while Roosevelt rattled off another four, all from Robinson. The big center was the only Panther to score that period, yet Roosevelt still led by twelve, 37–25, at the conclusion of the quarter.

After Keene opened the fourth quarter with a three-pointer from the top of the arc, Robinson and Harding each hit field goals in the space of a minute. Roosevelt's lead was 41–28 and Collinsville signaled for a time-out with 5:22 left in the game.

This time the time-out cooled off the Panthers. When play resumed the Kahoks outscored Roosevelt 13–4. Eight of Collinsville's thirteen points were scored by Keene, including another three-pointer. With 1:52 remaining the Kahoks had trimmed Roosevelt's lead to 44–41. Roosevelt's Antonio Lee was then fouled, and he stepped to the free-throw line for a one-and-one. He hit the front end, but missed the second. The Panthers were up by four and they called time-out with 1:27 left.

Collinsville's next possession saw Keene fire up a three. It clanged high off the back of the rim and Robinson soared to collect his twelfth rebound of the night. But as Roosevelt's Jeffrey Graham pushed the ball up the floor, Keene stepped in, stole the ball, and whipped it to Cavaletti who was fouled. Cavaletti stepped to the line for a one-and-bonus and sank them both pulling Collinsville to within two, 45–43 with 1:19 left.

Roosevelt ran twenty-one seconds off the clock before Lee was fouled with fifty-eight seconds remaining. Lee connected on his first free throw, but missed the bonus, making the score 46–43.

Collinsville's Kyle Jones rebounded Lee's missed shot and flipped it out to Keene who quickly pushed it down the floor. But just as quickly Robinson stole the ball, tossed it the length of the floor to Harding who laid it up for an easy two. Roosevelt 48, Collinsville 43 with forty seconds left to play. The Kahoks' Chris Reynolds then scored the last Collinsville points with a jumper in the lane. Harding answered with one of his own with twenty-three seconds left, and Roosevelt's Darryl Woods iced the game by sinking one free throw with two ticks on the clock to make the final score, 51–45.

Robinson and Harding scored in double figures for Roosevelt. Robinson had 21 points and 12 rebounds, while Harding had 16 points.

"We just got lazy in the second half," said Heflin. "They seemed to think it was over at half, but it wasn't. I think we played a good game overall, though. Harding gave us a lot of help, and Glenn was

Glenn, you know? He's gonna get his points. But Keene gave us trouble. I don't know what his stats were [24 points, 14 rebounds], but he seemed to be everywhere tonight. He's a fine player.''

"We got complacent," said Glenn Robinson. "We made some mistakes, and our defense let up in the second half."

Andy Elkins of Evansville Bosse simply put it this way—"We remember how it felt last year, we thought we really should have won that game, this year we want to go to state." That's how he summed up last year's memorable game against Bedford North Lawrence in the night game of the semistate. A game that many fans in the Evansville area believe was stolen from Bosse by referees bent on protecting Bailey.

With the three best players from that team returning for their senior year, including two All-State candidates in 6-foot-7 Elkins and 6-foot-5 Ron Darrett, Bosse began the season under the weight of some heavy expectations. Bosse's team the year before jelled in the last half of the season and by tournament time they were playing nearly flawless basketball.

But if it is true, as many say, that high school basketball is a guard's game, then Bosse's only significant weakness, the lack of a true point guard, could present a real problem.

Considering this fact, Bosse's opening game could not have been against a worse opponent. Thanks to Iben Browning's earthquake prediction for December 15, Bosse's scheduled opener against Henderson County in Kentucky was quaked out when Henderson County canceled classes. This meant that they would be opening in the St. Louis KMOX Shootout against nationally ranked Peoria Manual. Peoria had no one over 6-foot-2, no one significantly slower than Ben Johnson, and a reputation for forty minutes of vicious full-court pressing. To make matters worse Bosse's success on the football field, and some untimely injuries, tied up nearly every guard coach Mullan had, including starting point guard Brian Copeland. This allowed Bosse less than a week of full practice for the only team on their schedule that was simply quicker than they were.

"I'd be shocked if we won this game," Mullan said the night before. "They may have the quickest hands of any team I've ever seen." An indication of how bad things could have gone could be seen in Bosse's game plan. If they were having trouble getting the ball up the floor they would let Elkins try. Andy had grown from 6-foot-2 to 6-

foot-7 just last year, and had played most of his basketball at guard. He still had good ball-handling ability, good guard skills, and more poise than anyone else on the team. The idea was that Peoria would likely have their center guarding him, and Andy could probably beat him.

It didn't take long for Plan B to be put into action. Bosse opened the game with two quick baskets from Darrett and guard Antwan Pope, but Peoria scored the next four points off turnovers and the next inbounds pass went to Elkins. Crouched over protecting the ball, Elkins looked a little awkward bringing the ball up the floor, but he got the job done and scored 9 of Bosse's next 13 points. By the three-minute mark the guards had settled down and were handling the press well enough that it wasn't much of a factor, and the much taller Elkins was unstoppable inside. Bosse led 17–15 as the first quarter came to an end and a big sigh of relief came from the coaching staff.

Any relief felt by the coaches was short-lived as Peoria forced three straight turnovers to start the second quarter and immediately went on a 6–0 run. Elkins answered with a layup at 6:08, but the defense was collapsing on him now, trying to force Bosse's guards to shoot from outside. They were not up to the task and were unable to score for the next minute and a half. Peoria scored twice to take a seven-point lead and Mullan called his first time-out at 4:44.

Whatever it was he told the team Katrell Thomas must have gotten the message. At 4:34 he drove for a layup and was fouled. After a successful conversion of the three-point play and a missed shot by Peoria, he hit Darrett with an outlet pass resulting in a dunk. Nineteen seconds after the time-out, Bosse was back to within one at 27–26.

Peoria took a two-point lead into the locker room and what many had expected to be a blowout had turned into a good game. The 10 first-half turnovers by Bosse had been expected, and the guards had played well, but the team was obviously getting worn down, especially Elkins, who had quarterbacked the football team to the semistate giving him little time to get into basketball shape. What should have been a jubilant locker room looked more like an asthma ward.

Early into the third quarter Bosse was running out of gas. Unable to stop them from penetrating, Peoria went on 4–0 and 6–0 runs and Bosse could only answer one basket at a time. Not once in the period did Bosse score two consecutive baskets. By the 3:03 mark Peoria had taken a ten-point lead, and were showing signs of breaking it open. But Elkins, obviously exhausted, had resolved to keep his team in the game, scoring 8 of his team's 17 points in the quarter. A three-pointer by Derrett with forty seconds left cut the lead to seven, but Bosse looked as if they had nothing left to give.

The fourth quarter was a repeat of the third with Peoria answering every Bosse basket. Bosse's last gasp came three minutes into the quarter when they were able to cut the lead to six. But Peoria quickly ran off six straight points and when Mullan called time-out at 4:39 and down twelve, Bosse walked slowly to the bench. Most of the players' heads were down and those that weren't were looking anxiously at the clock. The Peoria players looked as if they were ready to play another game, and high-fives were exchanged by everyone. The rest of the quarter Bosse and Peoria traded baskets and the final score ended up 79–68.

But they had played well against an excellent team, and would not likely face anyone better in Indiana. In the pressroom after the game the quiet and reserved coach Mullan was almost giddy, unable to talk about the game without breaking into a smile. No coach with Mullan's experience is foolish enough to engage in games of "What if?" but surely he had to be thinking to himself, "What if we had had time to prepare? What if Darrett had played up to his potential?"

Losses early in the season have never upset coach Mullan, but this one left him as happy as any loss possibly could. In response to one reporter's question he summed it up best by saying, "I'm as happy with this team's effort tonight as I can be."

Shenandoah at Anderson
Saturday, December 8, 1990

The Wigwam. The Chief and Maiden. The North Central Conference. Tradition. That's the Anderson Indians in a nutshell. There are two other schools in Anderson—Highland and Madison Heights—and if you are loyal to one you despise the other two. But the Indians of just plain Anderson not only have solid teams, they have history and sentiment on their side as well, powerful ammunition for any high school program. And the folks at Anderson High like to flaunt that tradition just a wee little bit.

If you have never been to a game at the Wigwam, Anderson's homecourt, you might have thought, upon first taking your seat, that you wandered into some surrealistic opera rather than a high school basketball game. For while you sit there feeding your face handfuls of popcorn, the damndest show unfolds before you.

First, the opposing team, in this case Shenandoah, jogs onto the court under a rain of boos and catcalls. Then, the Indians run out onto the floor. The place goes wild. Now, running out ahead of the Anderson team is this kid dressed as an Indian. A huge, feathered headdress adorns his head and falls down his back, war paint streaks his face, he is clad in buckskin, he is brandishing a tomahawk, he leaps and kicks, and he is screaming his lungs out. The drums from the pep band in the stands pound rhythmically.

As the Anderson team warms up with layups and passing drills, the Chief moves to the jump circle at midcourt. Joining him now is a girl dressed as an Indian Maiden. A lithe, young lady, she is dressed in a buckskin dress that drops to around the knees. A headband circles her head. The Maiden kneels at midcourt, her hands on her knees, her back straight, facing the Anderson team. Behind her, standing very straight with his arms folded out before his chest, his trusty tomahawk in hand, is the Chief. Together, the Chief and Maiden keep watch over the team all through the warmups, barely moving a muscle, never cracking a smile. On this particular night, the Anderson team takes the wrong end of the floor for its warmups, so the two teams switch sides. The Chief and Maiden about-face.

Now it is time for a powwow. The Anderson cheerleaders and the Shenandoah cheerleaders meet at the circle at midcourt. They sit down in cross-legged fashion. The Chief hands the Maiden his tomahawk. She raises it over her head to show the crowd. The crowd roars. Then the Maiden hands the Chief a peace pipe. The Chief holds the pipe aloft in both hands and turns to the four corners of the gym, in dramatic fashion, and again the crowd roars its acknowledgment. Then he returns it to the Maiden who passes it around to the cheerleaders seated on the floor.

After the powwow, and after the two teams have warmed up and have returned to their respective locker rooms, the Chief and the Maiden go into their act. First, the lights are extinguished. Then a spotlight cuts through the dark and spills onto the floor. And who jumps into it? Why, the Chief, of course. Then the lights come back on as the Chief, and then the Maiden, strut and dance their way around the gym. The crowd eats it up.

When the Chief and Maiden stop dancing, onto the floor step the flag girls—enough flag girls to surround the entire playing area. The girls, festooned in boots and hats and feathers and garland, wave and twirl their flagpoles to the beat of a snappy march. Then the flag of the United States and the flag of Indiana are marched into centercourt by two more girls. They stand at centercourt surrounded by four other flag girls. The lights go out once more. A spotlight finds the American flag, the public address announcer recites the ''I am an American'' speech, the four girls surrounding the girls holding the American and state flags drop to one knee and snap a salute, and the band rips into the national anthem with an introductory fanfare that would make old John Philip Sousa grin in his grave. When the national anthem has been played the flag girls march out, the players return to the court, and they play a basketball game.

This goes on prior to every home game.

Here are some facts about the North Central Conference. The North Central Conference is made up of eight schools—Anderson, Kokomo, Lafayette Jeff, Logansport, Marion, Muncie Central, New Castle, and Richmond. Since 1981 the NCC has won the state title four times, and nine NCC teams have played in the championship game.

All NCC schools save one, Richmond, have won the state title at least once.

Of the three teams that have appeared the most times in the championship game, all are from the NCC—Muncie Central thirteen, Anderson ten, Lafayette Jeff eight.

Of the three teams that have appeared in the Final Four the most, all are NCC teams—Anderson seventeen, Muncie Central seventeen, and Lafayette Jeff fifteen.

The school that has won the most state titles is an NCC team—Muncie Central eight.

The school that has won the second most state titles is, how did you guess, an NCC team—Marion six.

The two largest high school gyms in the state are at NCC schools—New Castle 9,325 and Anderson 8,998. In fact, of the ten largest gyms in the state, five are in the NCC, the other three being at Richmond, Marion, and Lafayette.

When Shenandoah, from tiny Middletown, just down the road in Henry County, came to visit on Saturday, December 8, Anderson was playing host for the third of five consecutive home games. The night before Anderson had taken on Lafayette Jeff and had stung the Broncos 93–84. The Raiders of Shenandoah hoped to catch the Indians complacent after the big NCC win and perhaps pull the rug out from underneath a napping Anderson. And with 6-foot-8 Joe Reddy in the middle and leading scorer Joey McDaniel (11.8 ppg) out on the perimeter, the Raiders had a chance.

The Raiders made it a game for the first quarter and a half.

Shenandoah jumped out to an early 7–2 lead, with McDaniel popping in a three-pointer from the top of the circle. But Anderson responded with a 10–0 run of their own, spurred on by senior forward Shon Perry's 2 three-pointers and 2 free throws. The Raiders answered with a 12–4 run to end the first quarter up 19–15.

The second period started with a 4–0 Anderson run to tie the score at 19. After Shenandoah called time-out, Anderson took a 21–19 lead on a pair of free throws by Jon Cox. The Raiders tied it again with a pair of free throws by Reddy with 6:38 left. The two teams then traded baskets for nearly a minute. But Anderson took the lead for good at the 5:28 mark when guard Maurice Fuller hit both ends of a one-and-bonus to put the Indians on top 26–25.

Shenandoah managed to stay in the game until the 2:57 mark when McDaniel hit a jumper to pull the Raiders within 37–33. But those were the last points the Raiders would score in the half. The Indians went on a 14–0 tear, with back-to-back three-pointers by Fuller and Jason Townsend to end the half with a 51–33 Anderson lead. The only bright spot for Shenandoah in the entire second half was a 10–0 run midway through the last quarter when Anderson's starters had been pulled and the Indians enjoyed a 23-point lead.

Brebeuf at Anderson Highland
Saturday, December 15, 1990

With the graduation of Eric Montross, Alan Henderson became the single dominating force in Indianapolis. But even while the seven-footer was still at Lawrence North, Alan had always received his share of attention.

The senior year of a superstar is usually eagerly anticipated. When he gets to be a senior he will be at the very top of his game, and have the experience necessary to carry a team. That is the way it was for Glenn Robinson, and before him Bailey, Montross, Kemp, Austin, Edward, and Jones, and on and on.

When fans discussed Henderson's senior year, however, they spoke of inevitable disappointment. How it was such a shame that such a great player would have to play his senior year with no hope of seriously contending for any kind of championship. As a junior Alan had averaged 29.7 points and 14.3 rebounds per game, but only one other starter from last year's team returned—guard Greg Barber who had averaged 5.5 points per game.

Early in the season, IHSAA Commissioner Gene Cato and Assistant Commissioner Ray Craft sat in a restaurant in St. Louis before the KMOX Shootout discussing the upcoming season with some fans. Invariably the discussion turned to speculation on who might emerge from the various semistate sites—Evansville, Indianapolis, South Bend, and Lafayette. Out of the Evansville semistate most believed Bosse, Vincennes, and Terre Haute South were most likely to emerge. Roosevelt was the unanimous choice to come out of Lafayette. No one was sure about South Bend, maybe Concord, maybe Marion. Indianapolis? "How about Brebeuf?" said one of the fans. "No way," said Craft, "they don't have anything besides Henderson." Everyone else nodded quickly in agreement. "Martinsville's the team that will come out of Indianapolis," said Cato. To which everyone again quickly nodded in agreement.

As for Mr. Basketball, Henderson had the advantage of playing in Indianapolis, and his early commitment to I.U. didn't hurt. The problem was that Robinson would get a lot of attention by playing on a team that would be ranked in the top five all year. And it was very likely that he would be playing in the Final Four. This was the conventional wisdom throughout Indianapolis and much of the state before December 15, 1990.

But Brebeuf had messed things up by winning all of their games. Coming into the game against Anderson Highland, the Brebeuf Braves were undefeated with wins over highly regarded Carmel and Lawrence North. Tonight Brebeuf was to prove whether or not they really belonged among the state's elite teams. The Anderson Highland Scots would be the best team they had played to date and the game was being played in Anderson. Furthermore, Highland was the kind of team that would deal Brebeuf fits. Highland had a 6-foot-10 center, David Foskuhl, that, it was thought, could at least partially contain Henderson, and a 5-foot-9 dynamo of a guard named Randy

Zachary who had made a name for himself throughout the state as a freshman. Zachary was expected to have the Brebeuf guards for lunch.

Highland opened the game with a 6–0 run with Zachary scoring four of the six, but the slow pace favored Brebeuf. The Scots opened in a man-to-man, and when Brebeuf had trouble scoring they gave the ball to Henderson at the top of the key. When Foskuhl had to come out to guard him, Henderson burned him twice, pulling up for short jumpers to make it 6–4.

The game continued at its slow pace, with Foskuhl finally getting some help on Henderson. Highland finished with a 3–0 run to make it 9–4 to end the first quarter.

The second quarter was nearly as low-scoring as the first. At 4:59 Henderson hit a layup that started a 6–0 run that gave the Braves their first lead of the game 12–11. After a basket by Highland, Brebeuf freshman Larry Courtney hit a jumper to retake the lead at the 1:04 mark. Highland came down and looked like they wanted to spread the floor for the last shot, but Zachary found daylight and he didn't hesitate to take it to the hole. His basket at 0:45 gave the Scots a lead of 15–14 that held up until the half ended.

Henderson had only 6 points at the half, but he also had 8 rebounds. Not bad considering Highland only missed nine shots.

In the third, both teams started to speed things up a bit and Henderson became much more active on offense. Trailing 21–19 at the 4:00 mark, Zachary led Highland on an 8–2 run to give the Scots their biggest lead since the early minutes of the game, 27–23, and Brebeuf coach Mike Miller called time-out.

The Braves came out and immediately hit a field goal to cut the lead to two, but Highland played for the last shot, and got it. Highland had a four-point lead going into the fourth quarter, but Brebeuf had Henderson.

The truest measure of a star player is the ability to take over a game at crucial times and win it. Henderson measured up. He opened the scoring in the fourth by driving inside, hitting the layup and drawing a foul on Foskuhl. Although he missed the free throw to complete the three-point play, the basket sparked his team to an 8–2 run giving them the lead at 33–31, and it was Highland coach Alan Darner's turn to call time-out.

The Scots responded with some spirited play, as Zachary immediately hit a three. But every time Highland could grab the lead Henderson would take it back again for Brebeuf. Highland grabbed the lead for the last time at the 1:36 mark. After a Highland turnover at 0:32, Brebeuf called time-out and set up a play for Henderson. Their opportunity came early and the ball went into the big man with twenty-five seconds left to play. He missed the shot, got his own rebound and went back up strong. As the Brebeuf fans jumped to their feet, Henderson slammed the ball with authority, bringing the collapsible rim down as far as it would go. The Braves' defense held in the final seconds and the Braves came away with a 41–40 win.

They had beaten the best team on their schedule, and they had done it before a hostile crowd. December 15, 1990 was the last day that the Brebeuf Braves were considered noncontenders. The box score in the paper the next day was read in Indianapolis by Gene Cato and Ray Craft; and it was read in Martinsville by fans who, for the first time, now had reason to be nervous.

4

Radio

It's Friday night. The work week is over, and you're taking the wife and kids out for some dinner. Halfway to Frank's Steak House you remember that New Albany is playing at Charlestown.

"Damn," you mutter as you conk your forehead with the palm of your hand, you really wanted to see that game, too. But you don't panic. Instead, you quickly reach down and push the far right button on your radio dial, killing the golden oldie tune your wife is singing along with. Instantly, you hear the familiar voice calling the play-by-play at the Charlestown gym. You reach down once more to turn up the voice of Charlie Jenkins, not even daring to glance over at your wife who you know is staring daggers at you.

By day WXVW 1450 AM in Jeffersonville plays "The Music of Your Life," a format geared around the Big Band sounds of the thirties and forties. But on Friday and Saturday evenings during the school year Charlie Jenkins transforms the station into *the* voice for area high school sports. He's been doing it now for thirty years.

"The first game I broadcast there was a little guard named Louis Dampier who scored 36 points," says Jenkins. "Adolph Rupp was in the audience that night, and he signed Dampier to a scholarship at Kentucky after the game. That was the night of my very first broadcast."

That was in 1961 for a Seymour radio station. Since then the fifty-one-year-old Jenkins has won the Indiana Sportswriters and Sportscasters Association's Sportscaster-of-the-Year Award four times—in 1978, 1982, 1985, 1987—and has become the president and general manager of WXVW.

Jenkins began broadcasting high school basketball and football at WXVW in 1964. A year later Ted Throckmorton joined him as color commentator in the broadcast booth, and the two have been together ever since.

Tall and lean with thinning white hair, Jenkins greets you upon meeting you for the first time as if he'd known you for years. Without being the least bit presumptuous, he calls you by your first name and makes you feel at ease. You feel as if you have his attention.

Which is how he comes across on the air. His rich, clear voice is under control and rarely shouts, even during the roar of the crowd. His words are clear and carefully chosen, though without seeming to sound as if he were laboring to find the right words. Like all professionals, this man, who grew up in nearby Sellersburg, makes it look, or in his case sound, easy.

"My only concern is making sure that technically I can get on the air," Jenkins says. "Once I'm on the air my only concern is doing the very best possible job. I try to do the game as though I'm talking to one individual. It's as though you and I were sitting in the stands, and for some reason you can't see the game, and I'm just saying, ok, here's what's happening on the floor at this particular time. So I just try to do it from the standpoint of just letting one person know what is going on. To personalize it."

Sometimes informing that one person of what is going on isn't so easy.

"We are dependent upon a telephone line bringing that broadcast back to our studios," Jenkins says. "Many times I've worked almost to airtime to make sure my telephone line was up and running. One time in Evansville, when we were doing an Evansville–New Albany game, we went into the press box, and they did not have a telephone line for us. The telephone company had forgotten to install it. But there was a free telephone in the box, and for the first three quarters of the game we simply worked off the telephone just holding the telephone back and forth. At the third-quarter break, in the period of a minute, the telephone installer set up a loop at the far end of the press box. So actually in a minute we moved all the way from one end of the press box to the other, got set up, and didn't miss a beat. In all the years I've been doing this I've never—knock on wood—missed a high school broadcast. There have been times when I've come awfully close for one reason or another, but if we're to go on at 7:00 or whatever, I've always been there to broadcast the game."

In the three decades that Jenkins has been letting that one person know what's going on, he has seen high school basketball change somewhat.

"The biggest change since I've started broadcasting is the three-point shot," says Jenkins. "Teams can now erase deficits or create leads much faster than before. The players are bigger now, more physical, and the coaches have gotten better. I think that's because the coaches have been exposed through television and cable to more college games and thus more college styles. There are also more camps and seminars for coaches.

"The high school game seems to mirror the college game. If you see IU being very successful, then you see many of the high school coaches then develop that same style of play. Defense is a big part of IU's success; the high school coaches tend to copy that. We've also seen a lot of success in the last couple of years with running. The pressure offenses, the pressure defenses, up and down the court in the University of Louisville or Nevada–Las Vegas style. A lot of high schools employ that.

"I think, too, there is more strategy in the high school game at this particular time. The reason I say that is once upon a time a high school basketball coach might also have been the baseball coach, he might also have been the track coach or what have you. Now, the high school basketball coach can specifically gear all of his efforts twelve months a year to coaching his basketball team."

Jenkins also sees the growing specialization of the athlete, but that specialization being determined by the size of the school.

"I think the better athletes still play a number of sports," Jenkins says. "And in some of the smaller schools the coaches depend on the better athletes to play a couple of sports. If you go into a Salem or a West Washington or a Paoli or a Springs Valley you're going to see the better athletes playing both football and basketball. But in the larger schools the kids tend to say, hey, I feel my best sport is basketball so that's what I'm going to play. Most coaches work together pretty well, but there are some instances where one coach doesn't want a kid to play another sport. Basketball, furthermore, is almost a year-round situation anymore. The coaches want them in the open gym in the summer months working out, and getting ready, and a lot of times how well that kid does during the regular season depends on whether or not he was out running and attending open gym and all that during the off-season.''

Jeffersonville, New Albany, Clarksville, and Floyd Central are the four dominant schools in the Falls Cities area and are situated near the Ohio River about 100 miles south of Indianapolis. During the 1950s New Albany went to the State Finals four times, but never advanced to the championship game. The area teams went nowhere during the 1960s, but the 1970s were boom years. New Albany won the state championship in 1973, Jeffersonville went to the Final Four in 1972, 1974, and 1976. Floyd Central, dubbed the Superhicks, fought their way to the Final Four in 1971. In 1980 New Albany again traveled to Indianapolis, this time undefeated, but dropped the championship game to Broad Ripple to end the season 27-1. Jenkins credits the resurgence of championship-contending basketball in the area to coach Joe Hinton of Floyd Central. Hinton is flamboyant and sometimes controversial, and is the only coach the school has had since Floyd Central opened in 1968.

''Over the years my relationship with the coaches has been relatively good,'' says Jenkins with a grin. ''Take Joe Hinton, for example. I really like Joe. Joe's a unique person. Some people probably would not approve of some of the ways that Joe coaches, but he gets the job accomplished in his style which is different from a George Marshall [former Jeffersonville coach] or someone of that nature. I think that when Joe and the Superhicks went to the state finals, that sort of made people think that, hey, maybe someone from our area can make it to Indianapolis. Back in the 1950s New Albany went to State quite a bit, but there was a long, dry spell when no one from this area went to Indianapolis. Then Joe and the Superhicks made it to the state finals in 1971, and I think it made fans believe that there is more to it than just winning the sectional. Many times a team would win the sectional and they would feel they already accomplished everything there was to accomplish, and then they'd get beat the next week in the regionals. But Joe and his Superhick team made everyone realize that a team in this area could go to Indianapolis and be successful.

''Shortly thereafter New Albany won it all, and Jeff made it there several times. Really, the three years that Jeff was up there under Marshall they got beat by the team that eventually won it all. They got beat by Connersville and never should have. There was a disputed call on a blocked shot on the backboard. They were beaten by Marion with [David] Colescott, the Mr. Basketball that year. They got beat by Fort Wayne Northrup that had Walter Jordan who later played at Purdue. So I think that Floyd Central set the path in 1971.

"Probably the 1971 sectional was the finest sectional in total team talent that I've ever seen. Here you had Jeff with Mr. Basketball [Mike Flynn] who wound up his career flat on his back, fouling out of the game. You had the Superhicks with Jerry Hale and the Schellenburgs. And then you had the New Albany team that probably could have gone to the state finals that year. They had McCoo and Casper and those kids. That year was the best, but there have been a lot of great sectionals in the era that I've been here."

Jenkins credits much of his success in the broadcasting business to the behind-the-scenes work. Much like the athletes he watches and describes, Jenkins spends hours behind-the-scenes doing the little things that create success.

"I think preparation, like anything else really, is the key to being a good sports announcer," Jenkins says. "It is so important. The more prepared I am the better I can describe the play and the flow of the game for the listeners. But to keep up the enthusiasm for all that preparation, you have to have an intense liking of the game. You have to really like the sport.

"We try to stay in contact with the coach even during the off-season. We try to talk to the coach prior to the game for him to give us some idea of what to look for and so we can be ready for it when we see it. I have a pretty good rapport with the coaches and most of them will tell me if they have an injured player or maybe what they're going to do offensively or defensively, because they know I'm not going to go over to the other coach and say, hey, I just talked to this other coach and he said we're going to do this or we're going to do that. I never try to betray any kind of trust that we've been able to develop with the coaches. Over the years the coaches have confided in me, and they'll say we're going to use that offense or that defense."

Sometimes, though, all the preparation in the world is just not enough.

"As a young play-by-play announcer," Jenkins says with an embarrassed smile, "I did the Silver Creek Holiday Tournament one year. Now, I grew up in Sellersburg, and the correct phrase is 'deaf-mute.' But I never realized that was the correct phrase. Growing up, I always heard the phrase 'deaf and dumb.' So, there was a player on the Providence team, Gary Leonard, who was a deaf-mute. Well, Gary Leonard was having a great evening in the Holiday Tournament—just a fantastic evening. And I was really praising him, saying how well he was playing even though he had a handicap, that he was deaf and dumb. I thought I was really telling people what a great job he was doing. Needless to say his mother let me know that she was not pleased at all with me calling her son deaf and dumb all evening over the radio."

Despite such gaffes, Jenkins has earned the respect, as well as the confidence, of his listeners.

"I've had people call me up if a kid's been suspended and feel compelled to tell me the reason why," Jenkins says. "I've had mothers and fathers call me up and say, I just wanted to tell you, if the coach hasn't, why my son was suspended. This past season, for example, we had a game between Silver Creek and Jeff, and the Silver Creek coach was having a lot of problems, and he suspended this one kid, a really good kid, a junior, one game against Jeff. Now the coach told me what it was the kid was suspended for, but he asked me not to mention the reason over the air. So I didn't say anything on it. And so during the game I merely said on the air that the kid was undergoing a one-game suspension, but didn't say why. So the mother called me up the next day and she said, 'Charlie, everyone really enjoys your broadcasts, we tape the broadcasts, the kids really like listening to the games. Of course we had a radio in the stands last night and you talked about my son being suspended. I just want to tell you why he was suspended.' People don't need to do that, of course, but they do. I believe that's an example of the trust I've developed over the many years with the listeners."

Like many people in radio today, Jenkins grew up as a faithful listener to radio. Early on, he paid close attention to his favorite broadcasters.

"I grew up over the years listening to guys like Jack Buck and Harry Caray," says Jenkins. "I also listened to the Cincinnati Reds and Claude Sullivan. Over in Louisville was the old Louisville Colonels and a couple of guys named Jim McIntyre and Harold McTye. McIntyre later went on to announce for the Reds. These were men who not only were professionals, but who also exhibited great enthusiasm for the game which they broadcast.

"There are some fine announcers out there now who exhibit

that. Sam Simmamaker in Columbus at WCSI has been broadcasting high school sports for over thirty years. Morry Mannies from Muncie who does high school sports and who also does the Ball State Cardinals; he's done it for years. I think we're fortunate in the state of Indiana. We have guys like Hilliard Gates who announced high school sports for so many years. Don Fisher does an excellent job announcing for IU, though he doesn't do that much high school anymore. Bob Simmers at Jasper is a good play-by-play announcer. The fellow who died in the plane crash with the University of Evansville team, Marv Bates, was an extremely good announcer. He did all of the high school games in the Evansville area. He called the Evansville Triplets, too. In fact, NBC did a feature on him on the pregame show prior to a nationally televised baseball game one year. He was really very creative in doing wire recreation games for the Evansville Triplets."

Evansville, the largest city in southern Indiana, is on the Ohio River in the extreme southwestern part of the state. Southern Indiana is less populated and has fewer big towns than the central or northern portions of the state, and the poorer counties tend to be located in the south. Because Indianapolis, the media capital of the state, is so far away, many folks in southern Indiana feel their area is neglected by the more affluent and powerful north. This makes many southern Indiana Hoosiers feel as though they are the Rodney Dangerfields of the state—they get no respect. This feeling is especially strong among sports fans. When Larry Bird was playing for tiny Springs Valley in Orange County, for example, few people north of Columbus even noticed Larry.

"There is more coverage of the northern part of the state simply because there are more communities there, more radio and television there, and it's more populated than the southern half of the state," says Jenkins with a shrug. "I like to think that southern Indiana is competitive with central and northern Indiana, but there have been more central and northern Indiana champions simply because there are more schools up there than down here. And bigger schools. And no matter what you say, numbers are an important factor in any type of sport. Occasionally, we have teams that contradict that fact, but basically numbers are important.

"I think northern play is a little more physical, maybe more running. But I think the south has caught up with the north in the running aspect lately. Guys like Bixler, who came into Jeffersonville, have brought about a lot more run and gun. But basically I don't see a great difference between the two areas.''

A division between southern and northern Indiana may or may not be real, but a growing division between those who favor the current single-class system and those who favor some sort of special tournament for small schools is real. Commissions have been formed to investigate the feasibility of an alternative form of state basketball tournament.

''I have mixed emotions about how the state tournament is run,'' Jenkins says. ''I like it the way it is, but I do realize that small schools are at a disadvantage. There is something about the air of excitement of going in and doing the broadcast, and you've got 40,000 people in the Hoosier Dome. Where else would you have 40,000 people in a dome for a high school basketball game? And it's all because of the single-class system. The state finals is the culmination, it's the treat for a long season. I like that, but yet I realize the small schools are at a disadvantage and rarely do they enjoy that treat. I don't think there'll ever be another Milan that will win the state championship. But the memory of Milan is keeping the present state tournament schedule the way it is. Do you realize that Milan was nearly forty years ago? Breaking the schools into class would lose something. What I would allow the schools to do, I would let the smaller schools, say maybe under 500, let them go into a tournament of their own once they were beaten in the regular tournament. They would have to get approval, of course, from the IHSAA [Indiana High School Athletic Association], 'cause schools can only play so many games.''

Jenkins sees not only a class system as a threat to the success of Indiana high school basketball, but also other outside interests competing for the attention of basketball fans.

''The game is special,'' Jenkins flatly admits. ''There is a sort of aura around high school basketball that has developed over the years. Hopefully, we can keep that now with so many other activities, concerts, and teen-age work, competing against it. I think we are seeing a big emergence of girls' sports which I believe will pull attendance from the boys' games. A family can only support so many activities. Will they go to their one son's or daughter's games or to the other's school play?

''Basketball does have a special place for most Hoosiers. Why? I don't know. I think it is something that has just been passed down from generation to generation to a great extent. It's a simple game, really. Perhaps that's its lure.''

In the courtyard in front of the Indiana Basketball Hall of Fame, toward the bottom of the huge outline of the state of Indiana, is a brick with the following carved on it:

Charlie Jenkins WXVW
Sportscaster of the Year
1978, '82, '85, '87

''Radio has a public service to bring high school sports to the listening audience of a radio station,'' says Jenkins matter of factly. ''It helps create excitement, the air of anticipation, and I think radio compliments high school sports. Many times it is more interesting to listen to a sports broadcast than to watch it on TV. Radio allows you to use your imagination. You can make that player's shot however you want to make it in your mind's eye.''

Tonight's game, New Albany at Charlestown, is a classic big school-small school matchup with the small school having a legitimate chance of coming away with a win thanks largely to 6-foot-9 All-Star candidate Chad Gilbert. Charlestown is undefeated, but most of their wins have been blowouts against mismatched opponents. Tonight will be their first real test, and the first ''big'' game of the season for WXVW. All of the games broadcast so far have been of little real interest to anyone but the fans of the two teams.

Charlie Jenkins, Ted Throckmorton, and Gene Coomer meet at the radio station at around 5:30, and ride to the game together. This allows Charlie plenty of time for preparation, which he says is unquestionably the most important element of a good broadcast. They have been doing this now for the last twenty-six years, Charlie does the play by play, Ted the color, and Gene helps keep stats, rebounds exclusively.

''That's the way I like it,'' says Gene. ''That way I get to enjoy the game. Of course, they make me carry in all the equipment.''

''Yea, but somebody else always winds up carrying it back out,'' adds Ted jokingly.

''Let me tell you something,'' says Ted in a hushed voice as the smile leaves his face, ''you will never find anybody in this business that's better prepared than Charlie.''

And preparation is what makes a good sportscaster make it all sound so easy.

Entering the gym just after the start of the JV game, Ted and Gene are stopped by some people they know. Charlie pauses only momentarily, smiles, and nods his head in acknowledgment then keeps on walking, immediately seeking out the athletic director for Charlestown. After a few amenities, he requests four chairs. The athletic director escorts the crew up to a corner of the gym right among the fans to a small section where the bleachers have been removed, and after a few more amenities someone brings a table.

"Every gym is different," says Jenkins. "Sometimes we're in the corner, sometimes we're up high in the middle." The table is set up and an amplifier about the size of a large clock radio is unpacked. A small phone jack, just like the one in your house, dangles from an ugly, old, metal grating on the wall. The amplifier, needed for quality, is simply hooked in.

After twenty-six years, Jenkins knows the habits of the local coaches the way one might know the habits of a family member. Coach Miller of New Albany usually watches the first half of the JV game and heads for the locker room. About halfway through the second quarter Jenkins goes down to interview coach Cundiff. Before taping the actual interview Jenkins continues with the preparations. He double-checks the starting lineup with the coach, asks if there will be anyone who will see more playing time than usual, or if the coach will be trying anything different for this particular team. The interview, which is taped for replay just prior to the start of the game, is over minutes into the halftime period, just as coach Miller is heading for the locker room, the timing is flawless.

After the interviews are taped Jenkins joins Gene and Ted up in their corner. Some of the talk before the game is of the tendency for the Charlestown fans to get rowdy, and even during the JV game the gym is beginning to get loud. Despite the obvious potential for distraction, this doesn't seem to bother either of the announcers.

"When the game is exciting and the crowd gets going I think the players feel that and play better. And I feel it as well, and I think that comes through in the broadcast," says Jenkins.

With twenty-seven seconds left in the JV game New Albany is down two, and Charlie, Ted, and Gene are all pleading that it doesn't go into overtime. "No overtime, no overtime," Ted yells. "Don't foul 'em, don't foul 'em," but their prayers go unanswered—New Albany hits a ten footer with one second left to tie the game at 56. Even over the noise of the crowd, groans can be heard from Ted and Gene. Charlie laughs to himself and shakes his head.

"There's nothing worse than a JV game going into overtime," he says.

When the teams finally do come out onto the floor it isn't difficult to tell which is the small school. New Albany comes out in flashy warm-ups and performs layup drills punctuated by spectacular near-dunks and finger-rolls. After running a few passing drills, Charlestown starts their layups, there are no dunks, not even from Gilbert. It isn't often that a school of Charlestown's size has a legitimate All-State candidate, but when it happens it is one of the things that makes Indiana high school basketball truly special. The entire community rallies around both him and the team, feeling a heartfelt pride that few outside the state of Indiana could ever understand. Often they will write letters to sportswriters or take out ads in *Hoosier Basketball* magazine, all to promote their star. The crowds swell from a mere 800 to 1,800 or even 2,000, all holding their breath as the young man goes up for a shot, and each success bringing a sort of vindication. Any visitor who mutters, "He's not that good," or "He's not All-State," had better not do so too loudly, for this is their representative throughout the state and such remarks may as well be made about the town itself.

As the teams are finishing up their final warm-ups, the broadcast begins. Jenkins welcomes the listeners, tells them who is playing, the schools' records, etc., and announces a station break. The recorded pregame interviews are prepared and Jenkins listens through his headphones for the cue to hit the play button. Like clockwork the interviews are over just as the starting lineups are ready to be announced.

Most fans at one time or another have tried to cast themselves in the roll of an announcer. The first thing they usually notice is that it's not easy to immediately and fluidly identify the players without hesitation. "I wonder how they do it," they ask themselves. "Do they memorize every player and all the numbers?" As for Jenkins, he places two seven-by-ten-inch cards containing several large blocks with the players' names and numbers in front of him and just off to his right. The card for the New Albany players is in red and black, the school's colors. This, however, is really just a crutch, the ability really comes from preparation, concentration, and experience.

"Anything unusual about a kid you want to pick up on," says

Jenkins. "After one or two times down the floor I'll know the kid with the blue armband for instance, or the kid that's left-handed."

As the game begins Jenkins sits stoically with his hands clasped and resting on his lap, a score sheet on the table to his left, his watch immediately in front of him, and the seven-by-tens to his right. Jenkins' style can best be described as smooth and neat. Speaking rapidly but always clearly and steadily into the headset, he makes it all look unbelievably easy. During any kind of pause in the action he fluidly brings up the accomplishments of individual players, finishing his statement just as the ball is being swung around to the baseline for a jump shot.

As Ted jumps in with stats or an observation it appears as if they are reading from a rehearsed script, there are never any interruptions. Watching them, one can almost see and feel the twenty-six years of experience.

Ted's first observation comes shortly into the first quarter, and it is one that the Charlestown fans have already sensed—New Albany is very quick. Charlestown is having trouble even bringing the ball up the floor, and getting it to Gilbert is nearly impossible. The fans are becoming very nervous and the tension can be felt in the air. They had believed that their team could play with anybody, and now they looked as if they didn't even belong on the floor with New Albany, a team that wasn't even ranked. Six minutes into the first quarter, however, Charlestown had settled down, and thanks to some good outside shooting they were only down seven. They were only down seven and Gilbert hadn't even taken a shot, things were looking much better and the crowd began to relax.

At the 6:06 mark of the second quarter Gilbert hit his first field goal—a three, and it was about this time that Charlie's seven-by-tens had outlived their purpose. By now he was fully in the flow of the game, and his gaze only left the court when it was necessary to update the scorebook.

Charlestown had not closed the gap, but they had held their own, and with nine seconds left in the half Kyle Lovan hit a three to cut the lead to 34–29. The game was living up to expectations and the crowd had come to life.

Charlestown opened the second half the way New Albany had opened the game. Aggressive defense forced New Albany into several turnovers, and Charlestown was able to take advantage scoring the first six points to take their first lead 35–34 at the 6:10 mark. The crowd, which is right on top of Charlie and Ted, explodes when Charlestown steals the ball with the score tied at 39; a fan just to the right of Charlie produces an airhorn, which he immediately puts to good use. The gym has become so loud that several small children have covered their ears. Charlie's hands remain clasped in his lap, his posture betraying no emotion. Only by looking at his face can one tell that he is now yelling into the headset to be heard over the crowd.

The game remained pressure-packed until the end. Halfway through the fourth quarter, Charlestown forced three consecutive turnovers and converted on each occasion to take a 58–50 lead. The fans had gone from fervent to gleeful, and high-fives were exchanged all around. Charlestown was able to hit their free throws down the stretch and came away with a 64–61 win over big, bad New Albany. The fans had not been guilty of wishful thinking after all, their boys really could play with anybody, but as the crowd started to thin, a Charlestown fan turned to the man sitting next to him and said "I hope we don't have to play them again in the sectional."

Without the aid of a running score Charlie recapped the game for the listeners with amazing accuracy, detailing runs and spurts as if from memory. Coach Cundiff showed up for the postgame interview grinning from ear to ear. When Charlie asked him for his general thoughts on the game he said, "Well Charlie, I sure hope we don't have to play them again in the sectional."

5

Fire and Ice

Harrison vs. Bosse
Roberts Stadium
December 18, 1990

As the crow flies, Evansville is less than 150 miles from Indianapolis, but because no interstate directly links the two cities, the quickest way to get from one to the other is via Terre Haute—90 miles to the west of Indianapolis on Highway 70, and 120 miles north of Evansville on Highway 41. A quick look at a map will show that there are no cities of any real size within 100 miles of Evansville.

The feeling of isolation one gets in Evansville is real; it is like a small fiefdom, surrounded by various city-states like Princeton, Newburgh, Boonville, and Mount Vernon, and "the rest of the state" seems a world away. Not surprisingly it has developed its own culture. The nearest metropolis that most Hoosiers associate themselves with is Chicago or Cincinnati, and the Reds and Cubs are the teams of choice. In Evansville it's St. Louis and the Cardinals, and thanks to the success of Don Mattingly, the Yankees. All of this is so foreign to a visitor from another part of the state that it's easy for them to forget that they are still in Indiana.

Perhaps the best example of the separation that the people of Evansville feel, and one that is within the context of basketball, is the reaction of the city to last year's state finals won by Bedford North–Lawrence. All of southern Indiana feels a little overlooked when it comes to high school basketball, and that is why when Bedford won the State Championship all of southern Indiana felt a sense of pride and redemption. All, that is, except Evansville. To them even Bedford is "the other guys." Any feelings of neglect that fans in southern Indiana experience are felt doubly here.

Jim and Pam Stevens have sponsored an AAU in Evansville for the past six years. It is a testament to the wealth of talent in the Evansville area that for the last three years their Evansville team has beaten the Kentucky No. 1 team in an annual tournament held in Louisville. Every year the Kentucky No. 1 team is essentially the same as the all-star team they put together to play the Indiana All-Stars in June.

The Stevens have seen the best talent the city has to offer, and because of tournaments held throughout Indiana and around the country, they have also seen the best talent that the state has to offer. There is no question in their minds that the reason many Evansville-area players are passed over for the Indiana All-Star team is because of a lack of media exposure and, they feel, a bias against southern Indiana basketball in general. When players such as Brent Kell or Andy Elkins score 32 points against Princeton it is no more than a tiny number in a box score to most of the state, but when Marlon Fleming or Dewey Williams do the same against Noblesville it makes the 11:00 news in the Indianapolis metropolitan area.

This lack of attention has left many local fans with a sort of inferiority complex. When current Bosse assistant coach Brad Fraser coached the Evansville AAU team in 1989 he tried to spread the word about the best player he had ever seen in Evansville—Calbert Cheaney. Evansville Ace's coach Jim Crews also knew Cheaney was a special player and he was more than a little nervous about Fraser's attempts to broadcast the young man's talents. At the time, Cheaney was leaning towards Evansville largely because few major programs had shown much interest, and that suited Crews just fine. But as it turned out, coach Crews had nothing to worry about, no one would listen to Fraser. Local fans and even some coaches told him that Cheaney wasn't that good. It wasn't until Cheaney dazzled the scouts outside of Evansville in national camps and tournaments that the big-time Division I schools came calling. Even when Cheaney got off to such a great start at Indiana, some still said to Fraser, "Well, wait till the Big Ten season starts. That's when we'll find out if he can really play."

This year's candidate for most-likely-to-be-overlooked is a young man who deserves much better, a 6-foot-1 guard named Brent Kell. Brent is one of those rare individuals who, at the age of seventeen, has the presence of mind to see his own future and the discipline to seize his own destiny. To simply say that he works hard would be an understatement to the point of satire.

As a sophomore starting alongside Calbert Cheaney for Evansville Harrison, he began getting some attention from college scouts, but even before they approached him he knew what was going through their minds: "Is this 6-foot-1-inch white kid quick enough to play at our level?" He decided to answer in the affirmative before they could write him off as just another good Division II prospect.

He approached a friend of his who had done some work with the Harrison sprinters on the track team, and asked if there was anything he could do to improve his quickness. His friend told him about a new technique designed by University of Louisville basketball strength coach Doug Semenick called plyometrics—exercises designed specifically to improve quickness. Together they designed a one-hour workout employing plyometrics that had Brent in the gym every weekday morning at 6 A.M.

The grueling workout includes doing laps bounding on one leg, running using extra long strides, and suicide sprints. He "rests" between each drill by shooting free throws—an exercise in concentration. Coach Fraser, Brent's AAU coach, was amazed at the difference.

"Brent has always been a good player, but this summer, after that workout, he was electrifying every time he stepped on the court."

Any questions about his ability to play Division I ball were answered at the AAU tournaments between his junior and senior year where he impressed coaches from Niagra, South Alabama, Davidson, and Furman. "This kid would be a steal for us," said the coach from South Alabama.

Brent Kell's special gift on a basketball court, however, has nothing to do with his quickness or even his shooting ability, which is very good. It is an unshakeable court savvy, and an urgency to lead that makes him that special player of coach's dreams. It is this gift that has earned him the nickname given to him by Pam Stevens — The Ice-man.

"There are two pressure jobs in Evansville: Bosse basketball and Reitz football," says Bosse coach Joe Mullan. "You're expected to win." Coach Mullan has fulfilled his expectations; he is the winningest high school basketball coach of the 1980s. Not bad when you consider Bill Green, now the head coach at the University of Indianapolis, won three state titles from 1985 to 1987.

Bosse basketball is a tradition here; they get the best talent and the notoriety that goes along with it. Not surprisingly, they are also the most hated team around (with the possible exception of Memorial).

The odd thing about Evansville is that there are no long-standing rivalries—Bosse stands alone in basketball and Reitz in football. Basketball rivalries tend to be short-lived, coming and going between Bosse and whatever team is having a run of good teams. Currently, that team is Harrison, which makes for even greater drama because the Bosse kids and the Harrison kids largely come from the same neighborhoods. They know each other, and quite often, they hate each other.

Bosse entered the game ranked No. 6, and looking unbeatable. Six-foot-five forward Ron Darrett was coming off of a 47-point performance against Madisonville, Kentucky.

"He could have had 60," said coach Mullan, "he was on fire."

Ron Darrett's performance was a tremendous relief for coach Mullan, for he really was the key to Bosse's success. While Andy Elkins could always be counted on to give a solid performance every night, Ron Darrett was equally sure to provide the unexpected. He is unquestionably one of the most talented basketball players in the state, but he is also a wild card. When he steps onto the court he brings a tremendous amount of energy and emotion with him. When he is able to channel that energy positively he is unstoppable, like he was against Madisonville. But when he lets it get the best of him, he gets so hyped up that he can't seem to do anything right, like last year against Harrison.

Ron and Andy Elkins were also members of the summer's AAU team. One day during that summer, when Ron came into the gym for practice as he had so many times before, Pam Stevens noticed something a little different. He seemed very quiet, as if something was bothering him. A few minutes later, she learned from one of the other players that Ron's mother had recently died.

Pam immediately went over to tell Ron that he didn't have to be at practice. In fact, she told him that he *shouldn't* be at practice. Ron stared at the floor for a second or two, and without lifting his eyes, said, ''I got no place to go.''

Pam was speechless. Trying to find the right thing to say— anything to say, she asked if there was anything she or her husband Jim could do. Ron told her that he would just like to practice. And he did.

As the Indiana Hoosiers were lacing their shoes to play arch-rival Kentucky, and the Evansville Aces were preparing to make their first television appearance of the year, 4,000 fans sat inside Roberts Stadium getting ready to watch Harrison play Bosse.

The Harrison Warriors and the Benjamin Bosse Bulldogs were the heavyweights in Evansville, and fans had eagerly awaited the matchup. Bosse was led by Andy Elkins and Ron Darrett, both All-Star candidates. Although Harrison lacked such marquee names, they were also less dependent on any particular player. Led by Brent Kell and 6-foot-9 junior forward Walter McCarty, the Warriors were coached by Will Wyman, the son of legendary coach Gunner Wyman.

The opening tip went to Harrison, McCarty scored the first bucket at 7:22, and Kell hit a jumper thirty seconds later to give Harrison a 4–0 lead. Bosse answered quickly with their first basket at 6:09 and at the 5:35 mark Elkins slipped inside for a layup and was fouled. The big center hit the free throw to give the Bulldogs the lead at 5–4, and the game was shaping up the way the fans had expected.

The two teams exchanged baskets throughout the rest of the quarter with neither able to put together any kind of run. The first quarter ended with Bosse holding a 15–12 lead.

After exchanging baskets twice in the early going of the second quarter, Harrison went on a 10–2 run to take a 26–21 lead. Bosse committed three turnovers during that stretch and were looking completely out of synch on offense, but after a time-out Bosse responded with a 6–0 run of their own to take the lead back 27–26. Harrison answered with a goal by McCarty and then forced a turnover. With two seconds left in the half Kell hit a jumper to give Harrison a 30–27 lead going into the locker room.

During the halftime break fans with radios updated those without on the I.U.-U.K. game. In the outer arena a crowd gathered at the display case dedicated to the Evansville Purple Aces team that had died in the plane crash in 1978. And, of course, everyone discussed the first half. "Bosse played like shit," said a man of about forty in a southern drawl. "Well, you have to give Harrison a lot of credit, they played great defense, especially McCarty," answered his friend.

While debating exactly what had gone on in the first half, everyone in the stadium agreed on what would take place in the second. It would be a classic battle between two good teams, likely to go down to the wire. They were wrong.

What they saw in the second half was an unmitigated disaster. Bosse completely self-destructed. Harrison opened the second half with a dunk by McCarty that began a 10–0 run and gave the Warriors a 13-point lead at 40–27. Although this was not an insurmountable lead, Bosse's play during that stretch would have made a two-point lead look untouchable. Bosse finally scored at the 4:47 mark of the quarter, but during the 10–0 run Bosse attempted only four shots. Three of those shots were from within five feet of the basket and none had really come close. Bosse scored only 6 points during the quarter and the main thorn in their side was not Kell or McCarty but a little-used substitute by the name of Brian Spear.

Spear scored 7 points in the third quarter alone, and after Harrison had already run off 6 straight points, it was Spear who lined up a three-pointer with six seconds left in the quarter. The sound of Spear's bomb ripping the net was the sound of the final nail being driven into Bosse's coffin. The shot gave the Warriors a 51–33 lead, and the Harrison players raced to the bench all trying to be the first to slap Spear on the back or to give him a high-five. The Bosse players walked off the court shell-shocked.

As bad as the third quarter had been for the Bosse Bulldogs, the fourth was worse. Much worse.

At 6:50 in the final quarter Bosse had cut the lead to 51–37. A long rebound at the Harrison end of the court resulted in a loose ball that both teams scrambled for. It was one of those scrambles that seem to last forever. Every time a player appeared to find the handle, an opposing player would strip it away, and players would again go diving after the ball.

One player who nearly came up with the ball only to have it stripped away was Bosse's Ron Darrett. When the players again went diving for the ball, Darrett and Harrison guard Darren Winstead collided. A split second later Darrett got to the ball and his emotions got the best of him. Instead of grabbing the ball, he shoved into Winstead's chest. Both teams converged on the spot, and when Harrison forward Kevin Hardy tried to step in between the two, Darrett shoved him out of the way.

As the benches cleared, coach Mullan immediately hustled out to grab hold of Darrett. While the referees restored order, Mullan led Darrett over to the bench by the arm, lecturing him the whole way. The Bosse coach sat his star forward down, and never put him back in the game. Darrett finished the game with just 6 points on 2 of 13 shooting.

After each team sent a player to the line to shoot technicals, Andy Elkins tried to take over the game for Bosse, twice leading them on 4-0 runs. But every time the Bulldogs made a little run, Harrison's Brent Kell nailed a jumper to stop it.

With the teams exchanging baskets, and things starting to get a little mundane, a fight broke out in the Harrison section of the stands, and the game once again took on a lively air. Shortly after the fight a collision occurred under the basket and several players went down. All seemed OK except Andy Elkins who came up limping.

Elkins continued to play but his team was never able to get close enough to pose a serious threat and Harrison went on to win 73-62. After the game when Elkins was walking out to the car with his parents, he was limping much worse. His father had decided to have the ankle x-rayed just in case. No one expected anything more than a sprain, but considering the way things had gone for Bosse, the news shouldn't have come as a big surprise. Elkins had broken a small bone in his foot, and the early indications were that he would be out at least six weeks. Bosse could be competitive without Elkins but they could never hope to be a contender for the Final Four.

Coach Mullan was not nearly as upset about the injury as he was with his team. "All night we'd just throw one pass and shoot," said Mullan after the game. Not only had the players disregarded everything he had been trying to teach them, they had embarrassed themselves and the school by getting into a fight with the Harrison players. Mullan suspended Ron Darrett for three games which meant they would now be without their two best players in the upcoming Vincennes tournament.

The next day the team didn't even practice. Instead, a team

meeting was held. Coach Mullan had hoped that in the meeting he would be able to get his team more focused on what they were doing. Instead he listened to player after player blame someone else for the team's problems. It was clear that talent alone was not going to get the Bulldogs to Indianapolis. This was a team that had a very long way to go.

---—— • ***6***

Refs

From out of the corner of his eye the ref saw the kid from Portage come racing all the way down the court. He knew, he could just tell, that this kid was going to try to steal the ball away from the Kankakee Valley player, was going to try to swipe it away from behind. The ref also knew that the Kankakee Valley player was unaware of the Portage kid bearing down on him. The ref could hear a roar growing from the Portage fans, for they, too, knew what was going to happen.

The Portage kid was running with all his might, and when he reached the Kankakee Valley player he swiped at the ball. At the same time the whistle blew, and an arm went shooting up. The ref called a reach-in on the Portage kid. The hometeam Portage fans screamed bloody murder. So did the Portage coach, Greg Fisher, who called time-out.

"Are you gonna penalize a kid for good hustle! That's ridiculous! What the hell's the matter with you! Damn, that was a clean steal!" raged Fisher with his hands on his hips. Then he started coming out onto the floor, still jawing at the ref.

From out of the stands rained more abuse, faces red with anger, fists shaking in the air. Young, old, middle-aged, it made no difference, they all stood and seemed to lean forward in order to get just a little closer, close enough to let that ref know how they *really* felt. At that moment everyone in that Portage gym hated Steve Homner, referee.

Why? Why does one subject himself to such abuse? There are more relaxing and less stressful hobbies, you know, like collecting paper clips or watching the grass grow.

"You have to love the game," Homner said. "You got to love it or else the abuse, the wisecracks will eat you up."

When a coach storms out onto the floor, that is a no-no. Refs almost always slap them with a technical foul when they do so. But in this case Homner did not. He just stood there and ate it.

"In the back of my mind I knew I blew the call," Homner said, "so I just decided to take it. I anticipated it, you see, and that's one thing you can't do in basketball. You can't anticipate. Of course, you only got a split second to react, but you're supposed to see the play *then* make the call. And all that you're supposed to do in the period of one to two seconds. I didn't do that in that situation."

By day, forty-one-year-old Steve Homner is a mild-mannered insurance agent for Allstate in Chesterton. But a couple of nights a week during basketball season he turns into a zebra, running up and down a basketball court in search of that sneaky handcheck or that ambiguous blocking or charging violation. In the 1990–91 season Homner worked twenty-two boys' games and twenty-one girls' games. He has been doing it for nine years.

"I used to coach high school baseball at [Gary] Wallace," said Homner, a graduate of Gary Mann High School. "I worked there as a substitute teacher. When I left there, I still wanted to keep my hand in sports. I love basketball so I said, hey, why not get paid for it as well. So I got into refereeing. I just like doing it. Sometimes people don't like taking the abuse, but it comes with the territory."

Learning to take the abuse and learning how to avoid it being heaped upon you comes with time.

"You know when you've had a good game. You know it going off the floor, you don't even have to think about it. And you know when you blew a call, too. And if a coach is riding you on a blown call you're gonna sit there and take it. But the best thing that I've learned is that if I've blown a call, just admit it. Of course, I'm not gonna admit it if the game's on the line with three seconds left, but if it's during the game and the coach goes, 'Steve, he traveled right in front of you!' the best thing to do is to say, 'You know what coach, you're right. I blew it.' And right away they'll usually stop. You're showing to him that you're human, and that's usually the one line that will hush them up for a little while, anyway. Of course, if you keep saying you've blown it time after time, that isn't gonna work, either. But if you ignore them and act all arrogant they know that, too. And in that case they're gonna be just brutal on you. They can't stand that. They want you to be human. You gotta be human when you're out there. You gotta show that you're not God, and that's called court presence. I used to be cocky as hell on the floor, you know, I'm it, I'm it. But that doesn't work. Court presence comes with maturity, comes with working a lot of games."

But getting into refereeing, and more importantly, getting to ref at the varsity level and at tournament games takes more than sound judgment and a keen eye. It also requires some moxie.

You start out with the little guys, grade school and junior high games. From there you usually quickly move up to junior varsity games. It is the leap to the varsity level that is difficult, and there is no organization, no governing body, that will vouch for you or certify your ability. You have to go out to the individual schools on your own and convince them yourself that you are capable of refereeing a varsity game. You must hustle for a job, just like in the real world. Forty to fifty bucks for a varsity game, twenty bucks for a junior varsity game, twenty-five bucks top.

"You go to the coaches," Homner said. "Sometimes to the ADs [athletic directors], but usually the coaches. And you ask them for a job. If they want you, they'll call you. More often than not you have to follow up with phone calls and letters, and you have to keep on calling them and following up until they tell you to get lost. Be persistent, and they'll give you a game.

"But you've got to plant the seed. You can't just sit back and wait for the phone to ring. It doesn't work that way. I know JV [junior varsity] officials who will be working JV for the rest of their lives, because they do not have the initiative to sell themselves and go out and ask for games. They just figure, 'Well, I've done JV three or four years now, they'll start giving me varsity soon.' It doesn't work that way. Oh, once in a great while a coach will pay attention to you and hire you for a varsity game without you hustling for it, but that is a rare exception.

"I'll be honest with you. When I started out I told the coaches, 'Hey I think I'm a varsity official, no, I *am* a varsity official. I'll work your JV game, but if I'm good enough I want your varsity game.' If I did the JV game, and I think I did a decent job, I immediately contact the coach with a letter followed by a phone call then another letter. If another varsity official saw me and agreed that I did a good job I put his name in the letter as a reference. You gotta sell yourself, that's the name of the game in high school officiating. It's a selling job to get games and money. If you don't sell yourself, you don't get games. It's as simple as that."

Homner has yet to referee a boys tournament game, but for the past four years he has refereed girls sectional games.

"Yea, you get real pumped up for the tournament," Homner said. "They're special, and you look forward to them. You get a packed house, and let's face it, a tournament is a tournament and everything is on the line. That's when you are observed by your peers, that's when the coaches really take notice and they rate you. If you do a good job they see that and you have a better chance for work. It's good experience, plus it's fun."

It is even more fun if he is adequately prepared. Prior to each game Homner and his partner sit in the locker room and discuss those details that will make the game play smoothly.

"I like to know as much as possible about the teams that will be playing," Homner said. "What can I expect from these teams? I'll talk to friends in officiating and ask them what I should expect, and they'll say watch so-and-so in the middle he likes to hook or use the elbow. Or some such thing. Are they gonna be pressing most of the game, or is it gonna be a lopsided affair? Should I watch the coaches? Are they gonna be tough on us? Is it a rivalry game? If so, then should we take control of the game before any sparks fly? What it boils down to is that you have to adjust to the game.

"My partner and I go over a pregame plan. We go over things about floor coverages, who's gonna take the last shot and things like that. Although basically all the mechanics of officiating are in the book—you know, who's supposed to be where and when—we go over it anyway, or I like to go over it anyway. The reason being, that if the game comes down to a last-second shot or if it comes down to a play of who's got the charge or who's got the block, we're not gonna make different calls. You should go over that before each game, even if you've been out there twenty or thirty years. If both officials have a call, the under official is supposed to take it, all the time. If you got a last-second shot, the trail official, the guy on the outside, is supposed to take it. But you see a lot of things happen. Sometimes you see where the guy underneath is waving a basket good and the guy outside sees it no good and he's waving it off. Then you're really in a fix.

"And then there's preventive officiating. In other words we know this guy is gonna be jawing at us from the word go, and it's a good idea that when he starts, to just let him know that we're on top of it, and we're not gonna let him get away with riding us the whole game."

But the idea of officiating is to bring the rules to the game, not bring the game to the rules. Each situation, each game is different, and throughout each game things are constantly changing. The ref has to adapt to those changes.

"When I first started officiating," Homner said, "I thought, go by the book, go by the book and you can't go wrong. But sometimes you can't go by the book. Everytime you touch someone it's not a foul. You see, I thought it was all the time. The book says if you slap the backboard it's an automatic T [technical foul], but you gotta use your judgment. If a team's up by thirty-five, and the team that's losing, someone from that team goes up in the last fifteen seconds of the game to block a shot to prevent them going down by thirty-seven and he misses the block and slaps the backboard instead, hell, I used to call that a technical foul. Says so in the book, you see. They thought I was a nut. Sure enough I wouldn't get hired back from that school. I kept wondering why, wondering why, and then it dawned on me it was stupid silly calls like that."

Of all the officials Homner has run into over the years that have helped him with his officiating, only one has had the most influence on him.

"Bob Marcinak is the epitome of officiating," Homner said enthusiastically. "He's in a class by himself. He's over in the Hammond area.

"When I first came up I'll never forget it. I did a JV game at Andrean. After the game I came in the locker room, and I was feeling pretty good, pumped up, being a decent game and all. In he comes. Instead of just saying hello or anything like that he just comes over to me and he goes, 'Kid, get that damn hand up, straight up in the air. You're doing all right making the call, but you're not selling it right. Get that damn hand straight up in the air, look like a professional.' I didn't even know who this guy was. He said, 'You got a mirror at home?' and I said yea, and he said, 'Everytime you go past that mirror, get yourself in front of that mirror and stick that hand up, straight up, and see how good it looks.' I tell ya, everytime I saw a mirror I was pumping that hand straight up, and he was right, it did look good. I'd look at the other officials, and I'd see how a bent elbow looked, and I'd go man, that does look sad.

"Marcinak is the head of the Lake County Officials Association for basketball officials. He's also on the rules committee for the National Federation of High School Basketball. So he's there when they make all the rule changes, and he's there at all the officiating clinics helping you out. I've learned more from him than from anybody else. He'll go over the obvious things, but he'll just keep repeating it and repeating it until it just sticks in your mind."

Sometimes, when he is not working a game, Homner will sit on the stands and watch the refs, trying to find an edge, an angle.

"I've sat up there and watched games, and I'd see dynamite calls. But you still hear it from the fans, because they're all cheering for the hometeam. They don't care. It could be an obvious foul, you could hear the hands slap, and a foul will be called and they'll go, 'Oh man what a rotten call.' But that's just as much a part of the game as is shooting the ball. And I'm always looking for ways to improve my work.

"I love it, I love doing it. If you're out just for the money—and let's face it the money's not that great—believe me, it will catch up with you. Sooner or later you'd stop hustling and the coaches would see that and not hire you. Of course, you may not get hired back anyway. I've had times when I've dished out technical fouls, and nine out of ten times I'm not gonna be back to that school. That's horrible, but..."

Hall of Fame Tournament

New Castle
Saturday, December 29, 1990

No. 1 vs. No. 2. The dream of every tournament promoter. The Hall of Fame Classic, played at a different site each year, is the biggest single event in Indiana high school basketball other than the state tournament. The players it boasts make up an honor roll of Indiana basketball stars. It is easier to name the outstanding players that haven't played in it than those that have. Damon Bailey, Eric Montross, Woody Austin, Shawn Kemp, and Steve Alford to name just a few, have all helped to draw thousands of fans to the Classic. Every year the directors invite four of the best teams in the state to play, but only once in the thirteen-year history of the Classic has No. 1 met No. 2.

This is largely because it is not easy to predict which teams will be the best before the season starts. There are always disappointments, surprise teams, and of course injuries to contend with. As Mark Twain said, ''Prediction is very difficult...especially when it comes to the future.''

As fortune would have it, this year's field may be the best ever assembled, and that's saying plenty. No. 1 Gary Roosevelt, No. 2

Martinsville, No. 5 Mt. Vernon (Hancock), and No. 10 Southport bring in a combined record of 29–1, and the four teams are loaded with interesting and colorful players.

Roosevelt's Glenn Robinson, bound for Purdue, was picked by most national publications as the best high school basketball player in the country. Mt. Vernon's junior center, Brian Gilpin, had recently committed to Indiana University, but was something of a mystery to most I.U. fans. Many of them showed up for the sole purpose of seeing how he would do against Robinson, the best competition available. Southport's star was an electrifying 6-foot-4 forward named Marlon Fleming. For those of you who have never seen Marlon play just try to imagine Charles Barkley, only more aggressive. Martinsville featured long-range-bomber-extraordinaire Ryan Wolf, and big Bob Denton—a 6-foot-7, 290-pound All-American football player with a feathery touch.

Roosevelt was to play Mt. Vernon in the first game, Martinsville and Southport in the second. The matchup nearly everyone wanted was Roosevelt vs. Martinsville. No. 1 vs. No. 2. Big city vs. rural southern Indiana.

A No. 2 team had not beaten a No. 1 team since 1972 when Gary West beat Michigan City Elston 84–83 in overtime in the semistate. While Roosevelt fans may have found this encouraging, Martinsville fans felt the state was overdue for an upset.

The cars lined Trojan Lane more than an hour before game time. The games were to be played in the New Castle Fieldhouse, the largest high school gymnasium in the world. Less than a hundred yards away from the fieldhouse stands the Indiana Basketball Hall of Fame which had opened just this year. Most fans took the opportunity to visit the museum before strolling over to the fieldhouse to watch the games.

Although the Mt. Vernon Marauders (don't you just love that nickname) were the state's fifth-ranked team, Gary Roosevelt came into the game heavily favored. The Mt. Vernon fans were delighted when their team jumped out to a 4–0 lead and forced two early turnovers. Two minutes into the game Roosevelt had yet to score and Glenn Robinson had had enough.

After a long rebound Robinson broke to the other end of the floor, and when his teammate Carlos Floyd came up with the loose ball he hit the streaking big man with a perfect bounce pass. One player stood between Robinson and the basket—6-foot-11 rail-thin Brian

Gilpin. Fans inched toward the edge of their seats in anticipation as Robinson bore down on the slender Gilpin. The Mt. Vernon center did what any rational being in the universe would do, but what no good basketball player is supposed to; he got the hell out of the way. Robinson soared high above the rim and brought the crowd to its feet with a Dominique-like tomahawk dunk. The Roosevelt fans exploded and some actually started dancing in the aisles.

The play woke up the Roosevelt team and they turned up the heat on defense forcing four turnovers and outscoring the Marauders 12–4 over the next five minutes. But Mt. Vernon refused to fold, and in the last minute of the quarter the I.U. fans saw a little of what they were hoping to see out of Gilpin. With thirty-four seconds left Gilpin blocked a Robinson jumper, raced to the other end of the court and posted up on Roosevelt's big center. Guard Roger Huffman lobbed a pass in and Gilpin spun and nailed an eight-foot turnaround jumper over Robinson as time ran out to make the score 14–12 Roosevelt.

Gilpin had picked up his third foul during the quarter, however, and did not start in the second half. Robinson got the help he needed in the third as Darryl Woods hit four of six shots and forced two turnovers while committing none. This would have been the Panther's big chance to blow the game open had it not been for Mt. Vernon's 6-foot-8 center Chad Kleine who played like a man possessed hitting five of seven shots to keep his team close, and each of those five shots were big buckets. Roosevelt scored four times to increase their lead to five, and each time Kleine answered to cut the lead back to two. When Kleine hit a jumper at 3:20 he cut the lead to one at 38–37, but Roosevelt responded with a 6-0 run to make it 44–37. When Mt. Vernon's Chris White hit a shot at the buzzer to make it 44–41, the Marauders raced off the floor with momentum on their side and the feeling that they really had a chance to pull off the upset.

In the fourth quarter neither team was able to make a real run, but by the 2:23 mark Roosevelt had stretched their lead to eight, 58–50. It was then that Mt. Vernon made their move. First, Chad Kleine retrieved his own missed shot, scored, and was fouled by Tyrone Hunter. Kleine missed the free throw, but a long rebound enabled him to get his own rebound and score again to make it 58–54.

Roosevelt's Antonio Lee and Glenn Robinson both missed front ends of one-and-ones and Mt. Vernon scored again to make it 58–56 at the 0:46 mark, and things seemed to be turning their way. But Roosevelt showed they were not the state's top ranked team for nothing. As they had done the whole game when Mt. Vernon got close, they turned up the heat and pulled away. This time they did it from the free-throw line. Robinson, Ryan Harding, and Carlos Floyd all hit both ends of one-and-ones to complete a 6–0 run that put the Panthers up 64–56 with just thirteen seconds left to play. As time ran out, the Roosevelt players did little celebrating. The looks on their faces said, "We've got another game to win."

In the game between the Martinsville Artesians and the Southport Cardinals, Southport, after a slow start, jumped all over Martinsville in the first quarter. Trailing 6–1 the Cardinals went on a 12–0 run to make it 13–6, forced five turnovers, and held their opponents scoreless for the last four minutes.

As bad as the first quarter was, the second was worse. The Martinsville fans, beginning to feel the frustration, were getting downright belligerent with the referees, and to be fair, they had some legitimate gripes. They gave the refs a standing ovation that lasted a good twenty-five seconds when, at the 6:49 mark of the second quarter, they called the first foul on Southport.

Southport's guards continued to pass easily into the Artesian 3–2 zone and Fleming and forward Dan VonDielingen led a 6–0 run to make it 19–8 at the 5:50 mark.

After a Martinsville time-out the Artesians came out and finally started to play some ball. Three-pointers by Wolf and guard Chris Wilburn forced Southport to call their first time-out at 3:50 with a 22–18 lead that was beginning to look pretty shaky. Coach Bill Springer must have said something right during that time-out because his Cardinals came out and immediately went on a 6–0 run to make it 28–18. At 1:18 Bob Denton hit his first field goal to cut the lead to eight, but Southport answered with a goal of their own and with six seconds left in the half Marlon Fleming, Indiana high school's round mound of rebound hit a three-pointer to give his team a 13 point 33–20 lead going into the locker room.

Everything had gone Southport's way, and there probably was no one in the gym outside the Martinsville section that thought Martinsville had a chance to win. Most of the conversations during the halftime break were about a Marlon Fleming–Glenn Robinson matchup.

In the third the teams played about even, Martinsville outscoring Southport by one. In the fourth, a different Martinsville team took the floor. Although Southport still led 49–37 at the 5:21 mark, the momentum was shifting fast in favor of the Artesians. Martinsville came out and forced a very fast tempo and Southport looked ragged. The Martinsville fans were back in the game, and the players looked like they were on a mission.

Back-to-back baskets by Martinsville made it 49–42, and at the 3:19 mark Ryan Wolf hit a three-pointer and was fouled. Southport called time-out with Wolf heading to the line to make it 50–48. Wolf hit his free throw, but Southport responded after the time-out and went on a 6–2 run to make it 56–50 with 1:55 remaining to play. It looked as though they were going to hang on for the win after all.

After a basket by Wolf, Wilburn took advantage of a turnover hitting a three-pointer with forty-two seconds left to cut the lead to one. Martinsville had scored five points in seven seconds. After two free throws by Southport guard George Hemphill made it 58–55, Bob Denton snuck inside for a lay-up and was fouled by forward Brad Courtney. He hit the free throw to tie the game at 58 with twenty-seven seconds remaining, and with twenty-one seconds left Southport turned the ball over.

When a baseline jumper from the left side by Martinsville forward Chad Clements hit the rim and bounced over to the left side, there stood big Bob Denton with perfect position. His rebound basket at 0:01 gave the Artesians their first lead since the first quarter, and the game. The team poured off the bench surrounding their colossal center while he yelled to the Martinsville fans with his right arm raised high in the air.

Between games fans went either back to the Hall of Fame or grabbed a bite to eat and listened to the broadcast of the Peach Bowl where I.U. was playing Auburn.

The Championship Game between No. 1 Roosevelt and No. 2 Martinsville packed the fieldhouse. As the consolation game between Mr. Vernon and Southport neared its end, the Roosevelt fans and the Martinsville fans started cheering back and forth, each time louder and louder. When the Roosevelt team took the floor the northeast corner of the gym exploded with a burst of cheering and yelling. Twenty seconds later when the Martinsville team emerged from the locker room, the southwest corner exploded even louder. The atmosphere was like a Final Four, even the Mt. Vernon and Southport fans got caught up in the fun.

The tip went to Roosevelt and the Panthers brought the ball slowly up the floor. Perhaps it was nerves, or maybe it was just one of those nights, but the basketball that was played in the first quarter was downright ugly. Time after time Roosevelt would get the ball into Robinson, and time after time he would miss a turnaround jumper. For Martinsville it seemed as though every time Ryan Wolf touched the ball, he shot it, and every time he shot it, he missed.

At the 3:58 mark of the first quarter the score was 7–6 Martinsville, and this was from two teams that liked to run. After a television time-out, Ryan Harding hit a jumper to give Roosevelt the lead 8–7. It was the only shot Harding would hit in the quarter despite seven tries. Robinson went 1–6 in the quarter, and for Martinsville, Wolf was 3–9. At the end of the quarter both teams looked ragged, and Martinsville led 17–12.

In the second quarter both teams settled down to play some excellent basketball. After exchanging baskets a couple of times, the Artesians led 24–16. At 5:02 in the second Robinson drove the ball inside, went up, kept going up, and still kept going up until he was eye level with the rim. By this time it seemed as though Martinsville center Bob Denton had gone up and come down twice. Robinson jammed the ball home with authority bringing the Roosevelt fans off their seats nearly as high as Robinson had gone up for the dunk. This sparked an 8–0 run for the Panthers and tied the score at 24.

Martinsville came into the game with a reputation for having five guys that could really play. Immediately after a time-out following the 8–0 run by Roosevelt, Martinsville guard Chris Wilburn hit a three-pointer from NBA range showing the crowd that Martinsville was much more than just Wolf and Denton.

After a basket by Wolf, Roosevelt again went on a run, this time 6–0, to regain the lead 30–29 at 1:00. But in the final minute Martinsville was able to score four points and take a 33–30 lead into the locker room.

In the second half Martinsville packed a 3–2 zone around Robinson and dared his Panther teammates to shoot from outside. The Artesians went on a 6–3 run to open up a six-point lead at the 5:45 mark of the third quarter. From that point on, both teams continued to exchange baskets. Roosevelt hit eight times to cut the lead to four, and all eight times Martinsville answered to take it back to six. Back and forth they went like two boxers standing toe-to-toe slugging it out. Roosevelt got the last shot of the quarter with twelve seconds left and missed, but Robinson came out of nowhere, soared above the rim and threw down a dunk with ten seconds remaining to cut the lead to four 55–51 going into the fourth quarter.

Packing the zone around Robinson seemed to work. The big center had only scored four points in the quarter and no one for Roosevelt stepped forward to get the job done in his absence. After Rickie Wedlow hit one-and-the-bonus to cut the lead to 57–55, the Artesians spread the floor with 6:50 left to play.

As odd as the strategy may seem, it worked. Martinsville ran more than a minute off the clock until Wolf picked up his fourth foul at 5:39, and coach Tim Wolf, Ryan's father, called time-out. Ryan stayed in the game and over the next minute, trailing by only two, Roosevelt missed their big chance. The Panthers were unable to take advantage of back-to-back turnovers by Martinsville, and at the 4:30 mark it was Ryan Wolf that made them pay with a jumper just inside the three-point line.

After the teams exchanged baskets, Robinson twice went to the free-throw line for one-and-the-bonus, but could only come away with one point. With 1:30 left in the game Martinsville led 61–58, and big Bob Denton was headed to the line for a one-and-one. He could hit only the front end to make the score 62–58. Roosevelt brought the ball up the floor and the fans rose to their feet. With just over a minute to play it was crunch time. Every possession was crucial. It was No. 1 vs. No. 2.

Finally, after nearly thirty-nine minutes of basketball, a Roosevelt player other than Robinson showed his chutzpah and came through when needed. Panther forward Ryan Harding worked the ball at the top of the key and the Martinsville zone collapsed on Robinson. The closer Harding brought the ball to the basket, the more the defense collapsed. With a confident stroke, Harding went up for a 15-foot jumper from the right side, like he had been shooting them all his life. The shot hit nothing but net and the Panthers were down by two with 1:13 left to play.

Martinsville, the team that had spread the floor with a four-point lead and 6:50 left to play, then came down and promptly missed a shot with 59 seconds to play. Robinson ripped down the rebound and again the Panthers brought the ball slowly up the floor. One more time Harding worked the ball at the top of the key—51 seconds left—and as he brought the ball inside the three-point line—48 seconds left—the Martinsville zone again collapsed on Robinson. With 0:43 on the clock

Harding took the same 15-foot jumper that he had just taken, and the result was the same. The game was tied 62–62 at 0:41.

The Artesians set up their offense and when Chris Wilburn saw an opening he drove and was fouled by Darryl Woods. As Wilburn approached the line for the one-and-one, coach Heflin called time-out to try to ice him. But Wilburn calmly swished the first and after a deep breath and the subsequent embellished exhale, he swished the second.

Then, with the score 64–62 in favor of the Artesians, Roosevelt turned the ball over with six seconds left. As Martinsville guard Casey Walls streaked the other way, the Roosevelt players could only watch without hope of catching him in the time remaining. In that instant, they realized that they were no longer No. 1. Walls finished off his dash by hitting a layup as the game ended.

Big Bob Denton, all 6-foot-7, 290 pounds of him, bolted toward the scorers' table. The table for which he was headed was nothing more than the long table used in school cafeterias covered with a cloth. As he leapt up onto the table with both arms raised to the Martinsville fans in victory, sportswriters went scrambling, sure that the table would collapse. But the table did not collapse underneath the giant. He stood, still with his arms raised, screaming to his fans that were now the fans of the No. 1-ranked team in the basketball-crazy state of Indiana. For anyone wishing to know how it felt to be No. 1, Bob Denton's heroic pose visualized the feeling brilliantly.

Bob Denton had outscored the best high school basketball center in the country 19–15. Due to Roosevelt's poor outside shooting, the Martinsville zone was able to successfully shut down Robinson in the second half. In the third quarter he scored four points on two of five shootings. In the fourth he managed only one shot, and scored one point. It was the difference in the game.

In the new poll that came out the following Tuesday, Martinsville was No. 1 and Roosevelt was No. 2.

8

The Little Book

Scenario No. 1. You are in a bar in Anderson (perhaps the Spa, perhaps not) and some bozo from Indianapolis is trying to tell you that no one from Anderson ever won the Gimbel Award, the precursor of the Trester Award for Mental Attitude. In a flash you whip out "the little book" from your shirt pocket and show this moron that, indeed, in 1923 Maurice Robinson, from Anderson, was the recipient of the award. Humiliated, the guy from Indianapolis slinks away.

Scenario No. 2. You and your buddy are at a truck stop in Carefree, Indiana, down there along Interstate 64, wolfing down some chow before blowing into Evansville for the big Bosse game. All of a sudden, right in the middle of chomping on that chicken-fried steak, both of you forget where the Bosse game is being played. Is it at Bosse or at...who the hell is Bosse playing, anyway? Your friend blanches and breaks out in a cold sweat. Not you. With the confidence of Superman you reach back into the hip pocket of your jeans and pull out "the little book." You turn to the Bosse schedule and discover that Bosse...is not even *playing* tonight. It's *tomorrow* night. At Princeton.

Scenario No. 3. You are having a weekday "power lunch" with your boss. He's from Kentucky, you're from Loogootee. The conversation is basketball. Your bluegrass boss admits that your Hoosiers hold a substantial lead in the annual Indiana-Kentucky High School All-Star series, but no way, absolutely no way, he insists, has Indiana ever swept three-straight years. He'll even put money on it. "How much?" you respectfully ask. He slaps a ten spot on the table. With a grin that borders on a smirk you open your briefcase and remove, you guessed it, "the little book." Without saying a word you open it and point out to him the final scores of the 1974–76 games. As the blue-grass boy blinks his eyes, you palm the ten, and the conversation suddenly turns to marketing strategy.

What is "the little book"? Simple. It is a $5^1/_4$-by-$3^1/_2$-inch paperback book of approximately ninety-five pages that is an encyclopedia of information. Properly titled the *Indiana Basketball Handbook,* but commonly known as "the little book," it lists the schedules for every high school team in the state, lists the preceding year's conference standings, gives the date and location of holiday tourneys, lists all the state champions and coaches, gives the final scores for the championship game, lists all the Mr. Basketballs, prints the membership of the Indiana Basketball Hall of Fame, and prints the roster and schedule of Indiana University and Purdue as well as Ball State, Butler, University of Evansville, Indiana State, Notre Dame, and Valparaiso University. It also gives the scores to every game in the series between the Indiana and Kentucky All-Stars as well as the scores to every Indiana-Purdue basketball game. "The little book" gives the schedules for the NBA Indiana Pacers and Chicago Bulls, and it provides little known Indiana High School Athletic Association Tourney statistics, such as the state's largest gyms and what school appeared the most times in the Final Four (Anderson and Muncie Central, both at 17). *Everything* you ever wanted to know about basketball in Indiana is in there. For the true basketball fan it is like the American Express Traveler's Checks—he never leaves home without it. And all this for two bucks, if you order it directly from the publisher. If you get it from your local bank, where it is primarily marketed, it's free. But if you do try to weasel it from your local bank, hurry. It goes fast.

Meet David M. Pert, author and publisher of "the little book." Pert is seventy-five years old, stands about 5-foot-6, and is retired from a career in marketing. He never played basketball at Arsenal Tech High School in Indianapolis, where he graduated in 1932, nor at Purdue where he graduated with a degree in mechanical engineering in 1936, but he is on the board of directors of the Indiana Basketball

Hall of Fame. He grew up on Forty-ninth Street in Indianapolis and now lives in a lovely older home in the Broad Ripple area of Indianapolis with his wife of forty-six years, Madelyn. He has been putting out the book since 1968 and sees no reason to stop now.

"It's something I enjoy doing," said Pert. "I'm just a basketball nut."

Madelyn leaned forward and said, "Let me tell you this." She had a big smile on her face and was wagging a finger at her husband. She was wearing a purple jacket and matching skirt that dropped to her knees. The former schoolteacher and graduate from Southwest Missouri State obviously delighted in telling the story. "David had this dream he kept talking to me about. He said, 'Madelyn, as much as people love basketball in this state, I'd like to make something for them that they can put in their pocket and carry around with them. Something with factual information in it.' He talked about it and talked about it, and finally I told him if he didn't do it he would be sorry."

So he did it.

"I assumed," said Pert shaking his head, "that the IHSAA (Indiana High School Athletic Association) had the schedules of all the schools, but just didn't make them public. When I contacted them and told them what I wanted to do, they thought it was great. 'How was I going to get the schedules,' they asked. From you, I said. 'We don't have them,' they said. And Phil Eskew (former commissioner of the IHSAA) said, 'I can't believe you'll ever get it out, but if you do, I'll be the first one in line to buy it.' So Madelyn and I wrote the schools and asked for their schedules ourselves.

"Now, at first I didn't print all the state's schedule, just the schedules from the top hundred or so schools. But as word of the book got around, people would write and ask why wasn't their school included. So after the first couple of years, every school in the state has had their schedule in the book."

The market for Pert's book is the banks located in all ninety-two counties.

"I sell it to banks and financial institutions throughout the state," said Pert. "And in turn, they give it away to their customers. I travel thousands of miles a year within the state going to every bank in every county to sell the book. I have not sold it in all counties, but that is always our goal. Every copy of the book sold to a particular bank will have that bank's name and logo printed on it. But what with banks merging with other banks now, and banks being sold, I sometimes lose customers, 'cause the buying bank sometimes doesn't think it's worth buying my book.

"Now, early on, I used to print on the inside cover the schedules of the teams close by to that bank. For instance, a book sold to First National Bank in Valparaiso would have the schedules of the Valparaiso and Chesterton teams printed on the inside cover. But we soon dropped that. The book has evolved very nicely, but we don't get rich on it."

"He doesn't charge enough!" interjects Madelyn in mocked aggravation, nearly lunging out of her chair. "I always told him he didn't charge enough."

"But we make more than we spend," Pert says grinning. "Not much more, but enough. I wouldn't do this, nor would I have done so for these many years, if I didn't make any money from it at all."

The most difficult part of putting together the book is obtaining the schedules. Three hundred eighty-five schools are mailed red, yellow, or green flyers (the colored paper will stand out in a pile of white mail) announcing that it is that time again, David Pert needs the schedules. But the schedules Pert receives back in the mail are rarely in mint condition.

"We don't try to get the schedules, which is the hardest thing connected with the book, we don't try to get the letter out asking for the schedules until August," said Pert. "We contact each school by mail. If we don't get a response in three weeks, we contact them again. If we don't get it then, we go back again. After that, if we still haven't heard from the school we start making calls. But when we do get the schedules, oh, you should see them. Most are hand-written, and poorly hand-written at that, many have coffee spills on them, they're just a mess."

"Go get some of them that were mailed to us," Madelyn said to her husband. Pert scurried off to another room and returned shortly with a fistful of wrinkled, dog-eared sheaves of paper.

"Even when we can read them, sometimes we don't know what they're saying, 'cause they will abbreviate school names," said Pert leafing through the sheets. "Like New Palestein," he said pulling its schedule out of the pile. "They put down [on their schedule] that they're playing Eastern. Eastern who? Well, that means Eastern Hancock to them, 'cause they're in Hancock county. But there is a bunch of Easterns. There's an Eastern in Bloomfield and another in

Greentown. Now the people up in northern Indiana or down south probably wouldn't know what Eastern is being referred to, so we have to straighten all that out. We put the schools' correct name in the book, or at least the name the IHSAA recognizes. If we'd put that abbreviated name in the book how many people would know what school we're talking about? So now and then we have to call a school back and ask them what school are they referring to."

September, then, is spent typing the schedules and other copy in the proper format. And guess who types all 385 school schedules plus all the other typing necessary to ready the manuscript for the printer? And not on some fancy computer with a zillion bits or RAM or whatever, but on a *typewriter*?

"I will say this, the book is a labor of love," Madelyn said sincerely, her eyes flickering over to her husband. "And I love doing it, I truly do. Oh, it's hard work, I'm not going to tell you any different. We spend the whole month of September putting it together, but it's also a labor of love, and it's the kind of thing people want. It's something they care about. As long as he wants to keep doing this, I'll keep at it."

Madelyn confessed, though, that her typewriter is *electric*.

After Madelyn types the manuscript, it is sent to a printer.

"The book must be at the printer by October 1," said Pert, "and I have it printed now in Anderson. I have had seven or eight different printers over the years, some of those being in Indianapolis."

"He's very particular about how he wants the book printed," said Madelyn. "And I don't blame him. We put, he puts, many hours into it, and shouldn't he have it done the way he wants?"

"When we get them back, then they're distributed to the banks," Pert continues, "or people can write me for a copy. But I prefer they go through their local bank." For the 1990–91 book, 75,000 copies were printed.

The brainchild for the book might have been Pert's, but the production of the book is definitely a cooperative effort between David and Madelyn. When asked if she thought her name should appear as coauthor or copublisher, Madelyn quickly pooh-poohed the idea.

"The book is his baby," said Madelyn. "He thought of the idea, he brought the idea to fruition. He's the one responsible for its existence, not me. No, it's his baby, and he deserves all the credit."

"Let me tell you something about Madelyn," said Pert, nodding over to his wife. "We were down in Bloomington in 1972 [the state

finals were held in Indiana University's Assembly Hall in 1972–74].
Now Madelyn had not been to a tournament since 1954. She saw
Bobby Plump and that great game and she said, 'I'll never see anything like this again so I may as well not come back.' Well, I got her to
go back to the state tourney in Bloomington. We got down there about
nine or nine-thirty for the morning game. The game starts and she
takes off for a Coke or something. She didn't come back at the end of
the first quarter, she didn't come back the next quarter, so I went
looking for her. Well, I finally found her and there she was with a
couple of old basketball players, and she had the book out and she was
waving it around. They had been arguing over something, and I could
hear her saying over the top of the others, 'I've got the answer, I've
got the answer, 'cause I've got the book!' They had never seen the
book before, and I ended up getting orders for it right there as a result
of Madelyn. She talked to them for I don't know how long. They just
couldn't believe this lady would have the answer to whatever they
were arguing about.''

Pert's name is in the phone book, and he admits to getting calls at
all hours to answer arcane questions about Indiana basketball.

''I don't know if all those guys who call me are in bars or not,''
said Pert laughing, ''but I sometimes think they are. All kinds of people have called us. We've had Norm Sloan and even John Wooden call
us. Both of them wanted to know where they could get their hands on
a copy of the book. I don't mind the calls, really. If I did, I'd remove
my name from the directory.''

Pert knows of no one who produces a similar book in other states,
but he has had offers to make a similar book for other states.

''I got a call from a fella in Wisconsin to make a book for their high
school teams, but I wasn't interested. This one takes so much time
and effort I really don't have the time nor the interest, really, to do another one. There is a man out on the east coast, I think the Carolinas,
who makes a similar book for high school football, but as far as I know
I'm the only one making a book like this for basketball.''

Pert, too, produces a handbook for Indiana high school football.
Published since 1979, that handbook hasn't caught on as well as the
basketball book, and Pert said he might discontinue producing it.

But as for his basketball book, Pert speaks the truth when he
says, ''The IHSAA lives with my book, and so do a lot of other folks.''

9

Moving Towards March

Concord vs. South Bend Riley
Thursday, February 7, 1991

The South Bend *Tribune* teased the fans with a story that Shawn Kemp, who led Concord to the state finals back in 1988 and who is now a millionaire with the Seattle SuperSonics, would be present at the Concord-Riley game to help cheer his old team to victory. Shawn couldn't make it, though; he was busy heading down to Charlotte, North Carolina for the NBA All-Star Slam Dunk contest.

The tease wasn't necessary, however, for 6,383 fans jammed the Joyce Athletic and Convocation Center on the campus of the University of Notre Dame to see the fourth-ranked Concord Minutemen (13–1) take on the nineteenth-ranked South Bend Riley Wildcats (15–2).

It is safe to say that these teams do not like each other. Concord has had the upper hand in the last couple of meetings (Concord has won the last two games), and the Minutemen have dominated the regionals and semistate, going to the state finals twice in three years (1988 and 1990). Riley wanted to settle the score.

The Minutemen are led by 6-foot senior guard Jeff Massey (20.2), 6-foot-3 junior forward Donny Hackworth (16.4), and 6-foot-3 senior point-guard Mike Swanson (13.7).

The Wildcats, meanwhile, are led by a trio of senior guards: 6-foot Andre Owens (24.8), 6-foot-2 Eric Ford (24.4), and 5-foot-10 Scott Hecht (11.5).

The pregame press pitted a showdown between point-guards Swanson and Owens. But have you seen a Ford lately? Ford, as in Eric? It was a Ford and a Massey and a Taylor that put on the real show.

After the pregame festivities—which included the Riley team being introduced to a thunderous playing of the theme from the movie *2001: A Space Odyssey* and the team rushing onto the court through the vapor of several bellowing fire extinguishers; look out Anderson!—Riley quickly let Concord know that it was not impressed with the Minutemen's fourth-place ranking. Ford buried three jumpers from the right side and Taylor added four points of his own, and after only two and a half minutes of play the Wildcats were up 12–5. The Riley fans were screaming and a rattled Jim Hahn of Concord pleaded for a time-out.

It didn't do much good. Riley's Ford and Taylor each finished the quarter with eight points, while Owens chipped in another five, including a three-pointer from the top of the key. The Wildcats, too, forced Concord into six turnovers. Concord's Massey kept the Minutemen in the game by scoring 10 first-quarter points, including a three-pointer from the left corner. But Concord was still down by nine at the end of the first period, 28–19.

The Minutemen bounced back in the second period, though, mainly with the help of free throws. Thirteen of Concord's 24-second-quarter points came from the free-throw line, with guard Matt Stenden connecting on six out of six.

Riley's Ford and Taylor keep up the Wildcat pressure by scoring six and eight points, respectively. Riley continued to outhustle Concord, diving for loose balls and dominating the offensive boards, and with fifty-five seconds remaining in the first half the Wildcats enjoyed an eight-point lead. But the Minutemen rattled off four-straight points in forty seconds to pull within 47–43 at the end of the half.

The third period opened with a 6–2 Concord run, tying the game at 49 with 5:15 remaining. Riley's Bob Berger called time-out. That killed the Minutemen's run, and with forty-five seconds remaining in the third period the Wildcats took a 56–55 lead on the only field goal Taylor scored in the period. But Concord quickly came back with four points of their own, and it appeared as if the Minutemen would possess a three-point lead going into the final quarter. But Ford drilled a three-pointer from the left side at the buzzer to tie the game at 59.

For most of the fourth period the teams traded baskets. With forty seconds remaining, and Concord trying to hold a 73–71 lead, Massey clanged a shot off the rim and Riley got the rebound. The Wildcats charged down the floor, but Ford uncharacteristically hurried his shot and missed. Concord's Shane Bechtel rebounded and was fouled. Stepping to the line for his one-and-one, Bechtel's shot banged off the left side of the rim. A battle for the loose ball ensued between Concord's Swanson and Riley's Owens. Swanson came up with the ball and flicked it to Bechtel who got it to Massey who proceeded to step over the ten-second line under stiff Riley pressure. Riley ball.

With twelve seconds remaining Ford hit a three-pointer from the left corner giving the Wildcats a 74–73 lead and their fans a screaming fit. Concord threw a long inbound pass downcourt from Stenden to Hackworth, but Hackworth was fouled by Taylor on the attempted layup, and with five seconds remaining Hackworth went to the free-throw line for two shots and a chance to win the game. He missed the first shot, but made the second, tying the game at 74. Riley was unable to get off a shot in the remaining seconds of regulation. Overtime.

Overtime was the Eric Ford show. He sank a three-pointer, 2 other field goals, and chipped in a free throw to score 8 of Riley's 12 overtime points. The Wildcats outscored the Minutemen 12–7 in the overtime period, making the final score 86–81, Riley.

"We were very excited about this ball game," said a jubilant Bob Berger. "I'm usually watching "LA Law" about this time of night, but, hey, this is a lot more fun, especially since we won.

"They made runs, we made runs, and we were lucky to be ahead at the end. The kids knew the job they had to do, and they went out and did it. Ford was great tonight, but how 'bout that Taylor? He came through for us in the first half and with some big baskets in the fourth. I'm very pleased with his play here tonight."

Taylor, who averaged 5 points per game coming into the Concord game, finished with 22, a career high. He also grabbed seven rebounds.

Ford also had a career night with 37 points. Owens completed a triple-double; 16 points, 13 rebounds, and 12 assists.

Massey was the point leader for Concord with 28 points, 12 of which scored in the fourth period and overtime.

Elkhart Memorial at Michigan City Elston
South Bend St. Joseph at Michigan City Elston
Friday and Saturday, February 8–9, 1991

He is 6-foot-8, 220 pounds. He plays well with his back to the basket, and he can hit the turnaround jumper as softly as a kiss. He plays good defense. His only weakness may be a tendency to ease up on the offensive boards, to get blocked out. He is only a junior, but he is still growing. Major colleges like Indiana and Notre Dame are interested. Who is he?

Charles Macon has the body of a man and the face of a little boy. When he takes the floor at Michigan City Elston his face beams as brightly as the lights that burn down from the rafters. But opposing coaches are not fooled; rather, they seek to somehow draw a frown on that face, a frown of frustration.

John Wysong, the coach at Elkhart Memorial, tried to do that, too. Like most teams that play Elston, Elkhart Memorial collapsed three players around Macon anytime he touched the ball, and when Elkhart had possession they drove right at him in an attempt to draw fouls. The strategy drew the fouls, but it still didn't really frustrate Macon. Macon scored 19 points (8 for 15 from the field), grabbed 10 rebounds, slapped away 4 shots, and stole 1 ball to help the tenth-ranked Red Devils (15–2) to a 75–65 victory over Northern Indiana Conference foe Chargers of Elkhart Memorial at the Elston gym. The win also tied Elston with South Bend Riley for first place in the conference.

When Elston coach Dan Steinke sat Macon down at the 7:33 mark of the second quarter with two fouls, Macon had nine points, six in the first quarter including a three-pointer. After outscoring Elkhart 25–18 in the first quarter, the Red Devils managed only 14 points in the second while holding the Chargers to 10.

But after Macon sat down the Red Devils actually pulled out to a 14-point lead at 36–22 with 1:41 remaining in the second period. What happened? Senior guard Fred Holmes picked up the slack and scored 10 of his game high 21 points in the quarter, including 2 three-pointers. Seven of those 10 second-quarter points were in the crucial 9-2 Red Devil run that put Elston up by 14.

Macon returned in the second half to add 10 more points, and to give the home crowd a scare when he hit the floor hard and bruised his left knee with thirty-two seconds remaining in the game. The bruise was not serious.

But Macon and Holmes were not the only Elston weapons. Northern Michigan recruit James Williams scored 20 points, half of which were scored in the fourth quarter alone.

"That is what's so good about this team," said Steinke. "We have several players that can come at you. We're not one-dimensional."

It was actually a frustrating night for Elkhart's Daimon Beathea. The future Michigan State Spartan was held to 14 points, 8 below his average of 22.

"They're a good team," Wysong said of the Red Devils, "and they did a pretty good number on Daimon. I think they are underrated to be sure."

Macon fared better the next night, and his Red Devils won, but the young unranked South Bend St. Joseph team could not be put away until the final minute of the game, played again at Elston.

The Red Devils had no problems in the first half. Behind Macon's 12 first-half points and junior guard James McCoy's 10, Elston entered intermission with a 36-24 lead. During the halftime break the fans enjoyed the twenty-five-year commemoration of the 1966 Michigan City state champs. Many of those players from that team were on hand. They were introduced as they walked out onto the court.

The third period opened with what looked like a repeat of the first half as Elston raced out to a 9-5 run to go up 45-26, the largest margin of the game, with 4:28 remaining in the period. But after the St. Joseph time-out, the Indians outscored the Red Devils 18-9 to pull within 54-49 at the end of the quarter. Three 3-pointers by sophomore Peter Miller and another by sophomore Marty Harshman led the St. Joseph attack.

The Indians maintained the pressure in the fourth period. Senior Mike Berger sank a couple of free throws and sophomore Chris Quinn nailed a jumper from the right side to pull St. Joseph within one, 57-

56, at the 6:45 mark. Ten seconds later the Indians tied Elston at 58. Steinke called time-out, and the Elston fans were edgy. Where was Macon?

When play resumed, Macon went to work. He scored 11 of his game-high 34 points, 2 shy of his career high, in the last 6:34 of the game. Elston needed them, too. For with 1:14 remaining in the game St. Joseph was within two, 71–69, after Harshman drilled a three-pointer from the top of the key. But Macon replied with a smooth turnaround jumper with sixty-one seconds left to take the lead to 73–69. St. Joseph called a time-out with forty seconds remaining, but the Red Devils outscored the Indians 8–6 to put the game away and dropped the Indians to 4–13 on the season.

Macon ended with 10 rebounds and 2 blocked shots. As was the case the night before, Elston again had three players in double figures. Senior guard Herman Washington scored 17 points to go along with McCoy's 10 and dished out 10 assists.

"We did a pretty good job in the last two minutes of the game," said Steinke. "We executed to my satisfaction and we got some important boards."

Terre Haute South at Evansville Bosse
Friday, February 15, 1991

Tonight's game against Terre Haute South was exactly what the doctor ordered for Bosse. Despite having played some excellent basketball over the past several weeks, the misfortune of playing in Evansville meant that it had all gone largely unnoticed throughout most of the state. It is also likely that even some of the Bosse players still had some doubts about themselves. Terre Haute South was ranked eighth in the most recent poll and came into the game with a 16–2 record. They also had the notoriety that comes with having a player already committed to play for I.U. In other words, if Bosse could beat them, everybody in the state would know about it, and any remaining self-doubts would be eliminated.

Evansville Bosse came into the game at Roberts Stadium looking for its eleventh-straight win. They had won their last ten thanks to the solid play of their dynamic duo of Andy Elkins and Ron Darrett.

The Bulldogs jumped all over South from the opening tip with an aggressive man-to-man defense that kept the Raiders without a field goal for the first 5:20 of the game. Behind Elkins' six points, Bosse led by as many as eight in the first quarter. With 6:10 remaining in the second Ron Darrett stole the ball, drove the right side of the floor, drew the defense to him and scooped an alley-oop pass to Antwan Pope giving Bosse a 12-point lead 23–11.

After South coach Pat Rady called time-out, All-Star center Brian Evans, who will be playing for Bob Knight at I.U. this time next year, scored his first points of the game at the 5:52 mark of the second quarter on a three-pointer from the top of the key. After Terre Haute South's Jeff Hutz hit at 5:30, the lead was down to seven at 23–16.

The two teams then exchanged baskets twice, and then the Bosse Bulldogs went on a run. After a pair of free throws by Katrell Thomas, Courtney Dixon went to the line for a one-plus. He got the first, missed the second, but Andy Elkins simply outmuscled Brian Evans for the rebound, and went strong to the basket for a layup.

South guard Evan Mills was able to answer with a jumper, but the next trip down the floor Darrett, whose passing ability has always been underrated, threaded the needle with a pass to Elkins under the basket. Elkins went up strong again and was fouled. His shot danced around the rim and dropped through. When the 6-foot-7 center hit the free throw to complete the old-fashioned three-point play, the Bulldogs lead was 13 at 35–22.

During the first half, Bosse's defense had been its bread and butter. With a 37–26 lead going into the second half, the Bosse defense lapsed. Terre Haute South opened with a 9–2 run to cut the lead to four at 39–35. After Darrett took an inbounds pass and went up for a pretty dunk at the 5:34 mark, the Braves again went on a run. This time 5–0 to cut the lead to one at 41–40. After Darrett sank two free throws, Brian Evans lined up a three-pointer from just to the right of the top of the key and nailed it to tie the score at 43.

The Bosse defense woke up forcing three turnovers in the next two minutes. The Bulldogs went on a 10–0 run on baskets by Darrett, Fentress, Darrett again, Pope, and Dixon. After a layup by Evans and a free throw by Dixon, Darrett drilled a three with five seconds left in the quarter. Bosse again led by 12 at 57–45.

In the fourth South could do no better than to exchange baskets with Bosse, and at the 3:36 mark after Darrett completed a three-point play after being fouled, the Bulldogs had their biggest lead of the game at 67–53. Bosse spread the floor after Evans hit jumper at 3:21, and went on to beat the eighth-ranked Braves 71–59.

After the game Bosse coach Joe Mullan praised his team's defense. "That's about as well as we can play defensively. We're probably playing even better defense than we did last year."

The game was a very important one to Bosse center Andy Elkins. Most people in southwestern Indiana felt all along that Elkins was the best player in the area. Then suddenly, out of nowhere, it was announced that Brian Evans had verbally committed to play for Indiana next year. Elkins had signed to play with Evansville, and if he felt he had something to prove, he did.

Elkins completely outplayed Evans in the game—outscoring him 20–17, and outrebounding him 15–4. Once again, had a player from Evansville been overlooked?

Manchester at Northfield
Monday, February 18, 1991

If you went to the Manchester-Northfield game played on February 18 and arrived after the junior varsity game began, you had to park out on County Road 200 North that runs in front of Northfield High School, for the school parking lots were already full.

And if you thought you could just mosey on in and slap down three bucks for a ticket and park your behind anywhere you pleased, you quickly found yourself back out on County Road 200 North, probably listening to the game on WKUZ-FM and cursing yourself for lack of foresight, for the game was sold out. Jeez, on a Monday night, too.

The game was to have been played the previous Friday, but a storm dumped as much as eighteen inches of snow throughout northern Indiana that day, and over fifty games were canceled that night.

So the game was rescheduled for Monday, and the Norsemen of Northfield were laying for them. And not very patiently, either. Northfield was eager to avenge an earlier 85–84 loss to the Squires back in late December at the Wabash County tourney championship game played in North Manchester. It had been a tough loss, too. A loss on a last-second shot by Manchester's Mike Bazzoni, a shot many Northfield fans believe came after the buzzer.

Midway through the fourth quarter of that game Northfield held a six-point lead, and with only 1:24 remaining in the game the Norsemen led by four.

But with three seconds remaining, and with Northfield clinging to an 84–83 lead, Manchester guard Tony Freiden launched a three-pointer from the top of the arc. It missed, and junior forward Bazzoni scrambled with two Norsemen for the ball, wrestled possession of it, and tossed it back up. Swish, Squires win.

All in three seconds.

Well, things would be different with the rematch down at Northfield!

So, even during the junior varsity game, which is usually greeted with benign neglect at best, the Northfield faithful were raucous, cheering every Norsemen basket and booing every call whistled against their boys. And in the end, when the Northfield JVs posted a 35–24 win, the crowd of over 2,400 fans erupted as though the sectional had just been clinched. A final ignominy to the Manchester JVs was that with their final shot, a layup, the ball not only failed to fall through the net, but failed to come down at all, coming to rest, instead, at the back of the rim up against the glass. The Northfield fans got a hoot out of that.

So with their appetite whetted, the Northfield fans were ready for the evening's top card.

Manchester entered the game undefeated (18–0) and ranked sixteenth in the state. The Squires were only one of two top-twenty teams still undefeated, Washington Catholic (19–0) being the other.

The Squires could hurt you from inside or out. They were 45 percent from three-point range, and if you neglected the baseline or the middle, J.P. Pitts or Justin Pearson could cut for an easy two.

Northfield, on the other hand, was a respectable 15–4. However, fresh in the minds of Northfield fans was the 1990 team led by All-Star twins Joe and Jon Ross. The twins helped lead the Norsemen to the school's first regional title at Marion, and led the team to the finals of the Fort Wayne semistate where it lost 54–52 to eventual state runner-up Concord.

So when Northfield's Brad Hampton buried a jumper from the left side just thirty seconds after the opening tip-off to score the game's first two points the crowded, stuffy gym went berserk.

But that was the last Northfield lead.

In fact, the game was tied only twice at two and at four. It was

Manchester's game all the way, the Squires controlling the tempo of the game as well as the boards. Manchester's Pearson and Pitts grabbed nine and six rebounds, respectively.

Manchester was on fire from outside. Northfield's 1-3-1 zone was useless against the bombs Manchester was putting up. The Squires buried 12 three-pointers, with junior guard Bellows making 5, Freiden 4, and senior guard Jason Allen 3. All of Bellows' field goals came from three-point lands.

Five Manchester players scored in double figures. Leading the Squires was Bellows with 17, Freiden 16 (25 in the first game with Northfield), Pearson 14, Allen 13, and Pitts 10 (31 in the first game).

"This was our pace, this is the way we wanted to play," said a sweat-drenched Pete Smith, sipping on a cold can of pop. "It's nice to come down here on their floor and do what we did to them. Our first option was to pop the threes off screens, and I felt that was evident here tonight. When that option is closed to us we can revert to our second option which is to cut inside. We did that tonight, too. Balance has been our strong point all year, and it shows with all the guys we had in double figures here tonight. This was a much better effort than in the first game."

So was Manchester's defensive effort. In addition to allowing Northfield 15 fewer points than in the first game, the Squires also slowed down Northfield's ace, Noi Chay.

Chay, who unloaded for 42 points in the first game, managed 18 in this one. Jason Allen was the reason.

"Jason Allen was in complete control of Chay," Smith said. "He was Jason's man all night."

"Coach told me to stick on Chay, but not to get into foul trouble," said Allen. "My job defensively was just to try to slow Chay down. He's a great player, and he's quick. I think I did slow him down some tonight."

Chay was scoreless in the first quarter, but his Norsemen were only down 11–9 going into the second period. Manchester, though, opened the second quarter with a 7-0 run, and with 6:05 remaining Northfield was down 18-9. Coach Steve McClure called time-out.

Chay then went to work, scoring 11 of his 18 points. Having chucked the zone, Northfield went man-to-man, and Chay stuck to Allen like lint. Chay pestered Allen and managed a couple of steals, steals that the few Manchester fans on hand were certain were managed only by fouling Allen. But Chay's points included only two field goals, and teammate Brad Hampton was the only other Norseman to score a field goal that quarter.

The Squires, meanwhile, sank 4 three-pointers that period, 2 from Bellows and 1 each from Freiden and Allen, and when the bombs weren't flying from the outside, Pearson was cutting inside. The 6-foot-2 senior forward scored 12 points that period, 10 of which came from easy layups. From the 5:16 mark, when a Pearson layup put Manchester up 20-10, the Squires maintained a double-digit lead for the remainder of the game. The half ended with Manchester up by 12, 37-25.

The bright spot for Northfield at intermission was that four Manchester players—Bellows, Chad Lauer, Bazzoni, and Pitts—each had 2 fouls. But that bright spot faded as the Squires committed only 2 third-quarter fouls and easily outscored the Norsemen 24-17 in the third period. Chay fell silent, scoring only 4 points, and if not for Hampton's 9, the Norsemen would have been deeper than the 19 points they were down going into the final period.

Northfield did manage to bring the crowd to a roar when the Norsemen cut the Manchester lead to 15 when Chay drilled a three-pointer from the right side with 3:12 remaining in the game. But Manchester remained calm and fended off the late Northfield charge to win the game 80-69.

"We held our composure," said coach Smith, "and that pleased me a lot."

When asked of his thoughts about being 19-0, Smith replied, "When I was growing up, my high school went 20-0 during the regular season. We lost in the sectional. Undefeated counts only in the tournament."

Kouts at LaCrosse
Friday, February 22, 1991

When you step through the door from the outside and into the gym at LaCrosse High School, your first step is onto the playing area of the basketball court. When a player takes the ball out at that end of the court his butt scrapes the door.

The wooden bleachers are so close to the floor that errant balls frequently bounce up into the stands, occasionally hitting an unsuspecting fan in the noggin.

When a player approaches the scoring table to check into the game he must climb up five steps to do so.

When the Porter County Conference championship is on the line, as it was on Friday, February 22, the local fire marshal is concerned with the overflow of people—all 850 of them.

The LaCrosse gym, home of the Tigers, is a relic, an anachronism. Built three years after the *Titanic* clipped that iceberg, the "Tiger Den" seems more at home with the two-hand push-shot than with the slam-jamming of today's players. Indeed, thick mats hang on the walls behind each basket to cushion the momentum of the players who constantly fly by. About the only thing missing from this ancient picture is the narrow three-second lanes.

But thank the basketball gods that a place like this still stands. You will find here no fancy retractable bleachers, no state-of-the-art scoreboard, no slick weight-room off to the side. Just basic basketball.

And that was the bill of fare on the last night of the regular season. The Tigers, 17–2 overall and 6–1 in the Porter County Conference, were host to the Kouts Mustangs who boasted a 16–4 overall record and the same 6–1 PCC record. The winner would be the conference champ.

The two teams had already clashed once during the season. Kouts beat LaCrosse 64–55 at the PCC tourney back in January at Valparaiso. But coach Gaff didn't think that win was too relevant coming into this game.

"In the last game, we won, but that really makes no difference now," Gaff said prior to the game. "We're playing on their court now, and we'll have to give them everything we have in order to win."

Gaff was relying on a trio of seniors to provide the "everything": forward Sam Obermeyer (6-foot-6, 22.6 ppg), guard Greg Larson (13.9 ppg), and center Brad Redelman (6-foot-7, 11.8 ppg).

The Tigers, meanwhile, countered with senior center Scott Lawrence (6-foot-3, 20.8 ppg), senior guard Kevin Ketchmark (17.3 ppg), and Matt Gudeman (14.2 ppg). The Tigers were giving up height, but hoped to make it up with the shooting of their guards and with tough defense.

"I think one of the keys to this game will be how well we stay focused on the defensive end," said LaCrosse coach Bill Berger.

The two teams basically traded baskets during the first six minutes of the opening period. But after Kouts' Brad Redelman put the Mustangs up by three, 17–14, with a tip-in of his own missed shot, La-Crosse leaped out to a 9–0 run ignited by Mike Koselke's three-pointer from the right side. Ketchmark's eight points and Gudeman's seven helped give the Tigers a six-point first-quarter lead, 23–17.

In the second period the Tigers stretched their lead out to 10 points at the 3:07 mark when center Greg Lawrence hit a turn-around jumper to make the score 33–23. Both LaCrosse and Kouts turned up the defense in the quarter with Kouts forcing five LaCrosse turnovers in the period. But the Tigers' full-court pressure hampered the Mus-tangs, forcing Kouts into four TDs of their own while allowing them only 10 second-quarter points. Eight of those points came from Ober-meyer and Redelman. At intermission LaCrosse enjoyed a nine-point lead, 36–27.

Larson quickly cut the lead to six when he hit a three-pointer from the right side to open the third quarter. But Kevin Ketchmark answered with the next possession with a three-pointer of his own from deep in the left side. Redelman drilled a turnaround jumper at the other end to bring Kouts within 39–32, but again a three-pointer by Ketchmark put the Tigers up by 10, 42–32. LaCrosse stretched the lead to 11 with 1:45 remaining when Scott Lawrence sank one of a two-shot foul. But Kouts was able to cut the margin to single digits, 58–39, as the third period ended with guard Dave Hamstra sinking a couple of free throws.

When the final quarter began, it appeared as if Kouts might inflict the knock-out punch. The Mustangs roared out to a 10–2 run, eight of which came from the free-throw line. When Obermeyer sank the sec-ond of two free throws with 3:36 remaining, the Tigers were within one, 50–49.

But LaCrosse found the basket once more and went on a 10–8 run of their own to lead 60–57 with fifty-five seconds remaining. After Kouts' Larson missed a three-pointer from the left side with twenty-one seconds remaining, Kouts called time-out.

When play resumed LaCrosse's Ketchmark was fouled by Re-delman. Ketchmark went to the line for a one-and-one. He hit the first, but missed the second, making the score 61–57 with twenty seconds remaining.

Kouts inbounded the ball and under heavy full-court pressure managed to get the ball downcourt. They swung it around to Ober-meyer who was suddenly free as a result of a Redelman pick. Obermeyer calmly launched a three-pointer. Nothing but net, and the Mustangs were again within one, 61–60, but with only nine seconds remaining.

On the inbounds play Ketchmark was fouled. Calmly and quickly he canned the one-and-one to give LaCrosse a 63–60 lead with eight seconds remaining. Still there's time for Kouts.

Kouts' Tom McNeil was fouled on the next inbounds play sending him to the line for a one-and-one. He makes the first and intentionally misses the second in hopes of a Kouts rebound and quick field goal. But Kevin Ketchmark made the rebound of the game, going right around Obermeyer to grab the ball, and with that rebound sank the hopes of the Mustangs. Ketchmark was fouled and he went to the line to ice the game with his final two points. Final score, 65–61, La-Crosse.

For Ketchmark it was a career night. He scored 28 points, grabbed 10 rebounds, handed out 5 assists, and slapped away 2 shots.

"We wanted it real bad," said Ketchmark after the game in the locker room. "We were looking forward to this game, because of them beating us earlier."

Ketchmark scored 12 of LaCrosse's 17 fourth-period points, and 7 of those 12 points came at the free-throw line.

"I sort of got cocky out there at the free-throw line," Ketchmark said. "I just blanked everything out and did what I knew I could do. I must have been out on that floor a thousand times since being here, and it all seemed to come together tonight."

"My wife and I don't have any kids," coach Berger said, sitting in the stand after the game, accepting congratulations from a number of fans, "and every year these twelve young men are my kids. I love them. Ketchmark is the most unselfish player, isn't he? He'll do anything, do whatever it takes to win. He's been the money-man for a long time around here. He wants the ball at crunch time, and he always seems to answer the bell."

Someone asked him about the upcoming sectional.

"I'm not even thinking about that right now," Berger replied. "Hey, I just won the conference, man."

TOURNAMENT

10

Start of the Second Season

The regular season ended as it had begun; Gary Roosevelt (22–1) as the No. 1 team in the Associated Press poll. For the first time in the school's history, Gary Roosevelt had finished the season ranked No. 1 in the polls.

Roosevelt sat atop the poll much of the season. But after dropping a 66–62 decision to Martinsville back in late December at the Hall of Fame Classic, Martinsville captured the No. 1 spot. The Artesians remained there until February 12 when Roosevelt recaptured the No. 1 position. Martinsville had lost at Bedford North Lawrence on February 9, sending Roosevelt back to the top. In the final poll Bedford (19–1) finished second, while Martinsville (21–1) finished third. Alan Henderson and Brebeuf (19–1) finished in the fourth spot after being ranked seventeenth in the preseason poll.

Of the schools in the final Top 20 poll, eleven were not on the first preseason poll back on November 13. They were Washington Catholic (5th, 20–0), Muncie Central (7th, 17–3), Warsaw (9th, 19–1), Muncie South (10th, 18–2), Manchester (12th, 20–0), Michigan City Elston (13th, 17–3), Jeffersonville (14th, 17–3), Anderson Highland (17th, 17–3), LaPorte (18th, 17–3), Indianapolis Ben Davis (19th, 16–6), and Fountain Central (20th, 20–0).

The race for Mr. Basketball was a dual meet between Alan Henderson and Glenn Robinson of Gary Roosevelt. Here were their numbers going into the tournament: Henderson was averaging 29.8 ppg, 14.9 rpg, and 5.1 blocks per game; Robinson was averaging 25.2 ppg, 14.7 rpg, 4.2 blocks per game. Henderson was playing on the fourth-ranked team in the state, Robinson the first. Henderson was considered a more refined player with good ball-handling and passing skills; Robinson was thought more of a physical force in the middle with a great turnaround jump shot.

Brebeuf was considered a one-man show (Henderson), while Roosevelt could also count on Carlos Floyd or Ryan Harding. In a twenty game regular season Brebeuf averaged 70.8 points per game. Their average margin of victory for the nineteen games they won was 23.5. Roosevelt played twenty-three regular-season games averaging 78.6 points per game. Their average margin of victory for the twenty-two games they won was 23.6. Both teams lost one game each, Brebeuf to Ben Davis by eight, and Roosevelt to Martinsville by four.

Roosevelt played five teams during the regular season that were listed in the Associated Press Top 20 poll. They were Andrean, Gary West, Mt. Vernon, Martinsville, and East Chicago Central. In addition, Roosevelt played Gary West and East Chicago Roosevelt *twice*. So technically, Roosevelt played seven Top-20 teams, and won six. Also, Roosevelt played Collinsville, Illinois at the Coca-Cola/KMOX Shootout in St. Louis, the No. 1-ranked team in the St. Louis area.

Brebeuf played three teams in the regular season listed in the Top 20. They were Anderson Highland, Southport, and Ben Davis, and Brebeuf lost to one of those teams, Ben Davis.

Finally, consciously or subconsciously, academic performance would certainly be a factor in the decision among those casting votes for Mr. Basketball. Henderson was an exceptional student. He scored 1,300 on his Scholastic Aptitude Test (SAT) and was pulling down a 3.6 grade point average on a 4.0 scale. Robinson, meanwhile, struggled with the books, failing twice to meet the NCAA minimum SAT score of 700.

Going into the tournament, then, Henderson had four advantages on Robinson in the race for Mr. Basketball. He had better numbers, he played in Indianapolis, the media capital of the state, he was a model student, and he was committed to I.U.

The NCAA is not the only organization to televise the pairings of its tournament. On Sunday, February 10, the IHSAA televised the pairings of the eighty-first boys' basketball tournament.

Jerry Baker of the IHSAA network, Hilliard Gates of WKJG of Fort Wayne, Bob Ford of WLFI of Lafayette, and Mike Blake of WFIE of Evansville announced the pairings in a half-hour program televised statewide. Even cheerleaders decked out in full uniform were featured.

The sectionals would be held at sixty-four different sites from February 25 through March 2. The regionals would be played at sixteen sites on March 9. The four semistates played on March 16, and for the second straight year the state finals would be held at the Hoosier Dome in Indianapolis on March 23.

Starting in the 1991–92 season all sectionals would have six teams. This would be the last year for the four-team or eight-team sectionals.

11

Sectionals

Lowell vs. Kouts
Kankakee Valley Sectional
Tuesday, February 26, 1991

Never underestimate the power of revenge, especially in sports. There's just something about being beat, especially on your home turf, that makes you itch for a rematch.

So when Kouts drew Lowell for the first round of games at the Kankakee Valley sectional, coach Gaff saw an opportunity for a little payback.

"Well, the chance to pay them back did cross my mind," Gaff deadpanned.

Lowell had beaten Kouts 73-70 back on January 5 on the Mustangs' floor. Despite Gaff's three main threats being in double figures that night—Obermeyer with 25, Redelman with 18, and Larson for 14—the Mustangs were just unable to overcome a 17-point second-half deficit. Lowell had been on fire then; they were on a 9-0 roll, the best start in the school's history, and they had shot a blistering 60 percent from the field that night against Kouts.

What was frustrating for Gaff was that his team was so much bigger than Lowell's. No Red Devil player was over 6-foot-2. Kouts, meanwhile had the 6-foot-7 Obermeyer and the likewise 6-foot-7 Redelman. The Mustangs had taken it inside on Lowell, but still they couldn't get the job done. So a second try at them was good news for the Mustangs.

But something else was eating at their craw, too. Just four days prior to the Lowell sectional game the Mustangs had dropped their fifth loss of the season. Every loss is tough, but along with the 65–61 loss to LaCrosse went the loss of the Porter County Conference championship.

Kouts was not in a good mood.

A near-capacity crowd jammed the 3,887-seat gym at Kankakee Valley High School on Tuesday, February 26 for the opening night of the sectional. The host, Kankakee Valley Kougars, played county rival Rensselaer in the opening game at 6:00, while the Kouts–Lowell rematch closed the doubleheader at 7:30.

Both the Kouts and Lowell student sections were on their feet with the introductions of players. The Lowell students, as is the custom of many student sections, remained standing throughout the entire game. Kouts was designated as the visiting school and was introduced first. As Obermeyer, Redelman, Larson, and company were being introduced, the Lowell student section exhibited a bit of class by turning its back to the court and chanted "boring, boring."

The Lowell students were not bored for long. Lowell's Joe Rogers buried a bucket to score the game's first points, but Kouts' Greg Larson quickly answered with a three-pointer from the top of the arc. The teams traded baskets for the next two minutes. But Kouts' guard Dave Hamstra broke an 8–8 tie with a three-pointer from the top of the key with 5:50 remaining in the opening period. Thus started a 19–9 run that included back-to-back three-pointers from Sam Obermeyer, both from the same spot on the floor. Larson chipped in another five to go along with his initial three-pointer, and Redelman added seven of his own to give the Mustangs a 27–17 advantage at the end of the first quarter.

Kouts maintained their 10-point lead for only the first minute of the second quarter. In the next six minutes the Red Devils outscored the Mustangs 20–10 to tie the game at 42 with 1:02 remaining in the quarter. Troy Huseman sank both ends of a one-and-one to tie the game and then give the Red Devils the lead for the first time since their 2–0 lead at the start of the game. The Lowell run was fueled by guard Jeff Dillingham's nine points, and Huseman's seven. Lowell's full-court pressure forced five Mustang turnovers and allowed Kouts only one point in the final minute of the period. Lowell, meanwhile, managed four more points, all free throws, to take a 46–43 lead at halftime.

"I was very concerned at halftime," said coach Gaff. "I told the guys that we needed to bang the inside more. We needed to take fewer three-point shots and work on the height advantage we had."

The guys listened, but it didn't seem so at first. Lowell quickly went out on a 5–2 run, with Kouts taking poor shots from the outside. When Lowell forward Mike Piatt nailed a three-pointer from the right corner, Gaff called time-out with 6:25 remaining. Kouts was in the hole 51–45.

Kouts climbed back. Beginning with a three-pointer by Larson the Mustangs went on a 9–0 run, taking a 54–51 lead with 4:25 remaining. After Lowell scored the next four points, Kouts hit another run, this time a 6–0 run to take a 60–55 lead with 1:47 left in the quarter. In that 15-point run, Obermeyer was everywhere, hitting soft turnaround jumpers down low and kissing the ball off the glass for easy layups. When the quarter was up Obermeyer had scored 10 points, as many as he scored the entire first half.

The final period began with Kouts nursing a 62–59 lead. It didn't last long. Lowell raced out to a 7–0 run, and when Red Devil Jeff Dillingham buried a three-pointer from the right corner Kouts called a time-out with 6:30 remaining and down 66–62.

When play resumed Lowell stretched their lead to five when Dillingham connected on one of a one-and-one. But Kouts wouldn't go down. Hamstra hit the front end of a one-and-one, Obermeyer connected on a turnaround jumper in the middle, and Tom McNeil tied the game at 67 with 5:07 remaining in the game with a tip-in of his own missed shot. The Obermeyer, who else, drilled another bucket from the corner to finish a 7–1 run that gave the Mustangs the lead for good with 4:30 remaining.

Lowell, though, wasn't finished. Kouts hit their last field goal of the game at 2:55 when Obermeyer scored from the near-right side. Then Lowell's Mike Piatt connected for a field goal and a three-pointer, and Huseman hit a jumper to pull the Red Devils to within two, 78–76, with only 1:18 left. Kouts signaled for a time-out to talk it all over.

But money talks, and in Kouts' case Obermeyer is money. Money went to the foul line eight times in the last sixty-three seconds of the game and scored eight points. Hamstra visited the line three times during that same sixty-three seconds and came away with two points. When the "boring" game finally ran out of time, Kouts owned an 88–79 victory.

"I felt like we didn't have it in the bag until seven seconds were left," said a smiling and relieved Marty Gaff. "This was a game of spurts. Each side seemed to thrive on little runs. And, of course, Sam came through down the stretch. This was a big night for him. But a lot of credit, too, has to go to our guards, especially Hamstra. He had some nice touches out there tonight."

A lot of those "touches" came from the free-throw line. Kouts fired up only two fewer free throws than field goals. Of the Mustangs' 88 points, 33 came from the free-throw line; they shot 47 free throws (70 percent). From the field, meanwhile, Kouts put up 49 attempts connecting on 25 (51 percent).

Lowell, on the other hand, only went to the line 18 times, connecting for 13 (72 percent). For both Kouts–Lowell games, Kouts shot 68 free throws to Lowell's 32.

But the sectional matchup between these two teams was truly the Sam Obermeyer show. He scored a career-high 36 points (26 in the second half, 16 in the fourth period, 12 from the free-throw line, 2 three-pointers), 14 rebounds (evenly split between offensive and defensive), two block shots, and a steal.

"This is the best emotional feeling in the locker room we've had all year," said the lanky, baby-faced Obermeyer. "We wanted it real bad tonight, and the guys did a good job getting the ball to me. I was just hot tonight."

Four of Kouts' starting five scored in double figures. In addition to Obermeyers' 36, Redelman scored 16, Larson 15, and McNeil 10.

It was a good start.

Rensselaer vs. Kouts
Kankakee Valley Sectional Semifinal
Friday, March 1, 1991

Only once in the school's history has Kouts ever won the sectional, and that was back in 1987, a team coached by the current Kouts coach, Marty Gaff.

Now Gaff's Mustangs faced the Rensselaer Bombers in the semi-finals of the Kankakee Valley sectional, and Gaff believed the winner of that game would be the eventual champion of the sectional. Gaff felt his team had a good chance of claiming another sectional championship for Kouts, too. He had inside height with Obermeyer, Redelman, and McNeil, and he had some outside shooting and ball-handling in Larson and Hamstra. Now, if they could just get past these Bombers...

Rensselaer, an easy 63–48 winner over Kankakee Valley in the opening game of the sectional, presented a different problem for Kouts than did Lowell. Lowell's front line had not been nearly as big as Kouts', and the Mustangs had had an easy job of getting the ball inside to Obermeyer and Redelman, as witness their 36 and 16 points, respectively.

Rensselaer, on the other hand, had a big front line of its own. Senior center Steve Gehring was 6-foot-6, sophomore forward Ryan Hooker was 6-foot-4, and senior forward Dan Brandenburg was 6-foot-3. And they had a pesky guard named Clint Swan who swarmed all around the perimeter with the bad habit of sinking jumpers. And, whereas Kouts was hungry for a sectional win, Rensselaer was downright famished. It had *never* won a sectional championship at Kankakee Valley, and their last sectional victory had been a 52–50 squeaker over Benton Central at North Newton only weeks after Richard Nixon had been sworn in for his first term as president.

Kankakee Valley High School is located in Wheatfield in northern Jasper county, and Rensselaer, some twenty miles south, is the county seat. So the bleachers were a noisy sea of red and black, Rensselaer's colors, when the two teams shook hands at centercourt.

The Bombers got the tip, and ten seconds later Clint Swan lobbed a pass over Kouts' 3-2 zone to Steve Gehring for an easy two points. A minute later Kouts' Tom McNeil tipped in an errant three-pointer from Obermeyer to tie the game. Those two possessions quickly set the tone of the game: Rensselaer was not intimidated with Kouts' height, and the Bombers were not going to allow the Mustangs inside, but were forcing them to score from the outside.

Dan Brandenburg tied the game at 10 with a two-handed stuff, the first of the sectional, with 2:47 remaining in the opening quarter. Then Gehring added another layup to go up 12–10. Thirty seconds later Brandenburg again moved hard to the bucket for an apparent jam, but Obermeyer slipped in to prevent the slam, yet was unable to stop the bucket. Obermeyer was charged with a foul, his second, and Brandenburg converted the free throw to give the Bombers a 15–10 lead with 1:22 remaining in the opening quarter. Obermeyer stayed in the game.

After Redelman sank the front end of a one-and-one to start the second quarter, Rensselaer rattled off four quick points, again easy layups. Kouts called time-out with 6:48 remaining, trailing 19–13.

The Mustangs returned to the floor with possession of the ball and Obermeyer nailed a three-pointer from the right side. Kouts fell back into a man-to-man defense in the hope of stopping Rensselaer from going inside. It worked, so the Bombers simply went outside. The ball was kicked out to Swan who calmly sank a three-pointer of his own from the right side. The lead was still six, 22–16.

But with three straight baskets from Redelman, Larson, and Obermeyer, Kouts tied the game at 22 with fifty-nine seconds left in the half. Rensselaer's Jacob Chapman scored on a jumper at the free-throw line with thirty-one seconds left. Kouts came down the floor quickly and Redelman drove the lane for what appeared to be an easy layup to tie the game, but the ball rolled off the rim to the left side. The Bombers grabbed the rebound, and with ten seconds showing on the clock Brandon Cain hit a jumper from the right side. The Mustangs' last-second shot was way off the mark, and Rensselaer entered the halftime locker room with a 26–22 advantage.

Though they led at the half, the Bombers were a bit puzzled as to why their lead was not more than four. Rensselaer had forced Kouts into 11 first-half turnovers, had gone to the free-throw line 8 times to Kouts' 4, and had held Obermeyer and Redelman to a combined 8 points. Rensselaer's defense was working; they just needed a little offensive power to finish them off.

The third quarter didn't provide it for the Bombers. Kouts roared out to an 11–2 run to start the second half. The run started and ended with Obermeyer. He opened the run by sinking both ends of a two-shot foul. After Swan hit a jumper from the right side, Tom McNeil tipped in a missed Redelman jumper, then came right back twenty seconds later to score on a layup. After Swan missed down at the other end, Kouts came down the floor and swung it over to Obermeyer who drilled a three-pointer from the top of the arc. On the subsequent Rensselaer inbounds play, Obermeyer stole the ball and stuffed it home. The Mustangs' fans erupted, and the Bombers called time-out with 5:42 remaining and trailing 33–28.

Obermeyer picked up his third foul with 4:56 remaining, but stayed in the game. His foul resulted in no Bomber points.

Brandenburg scored underneath for the Bombers on the first play after resumption of play. But Larson answered with a three-pointer from the left corner. Rensselaer failed to score on their next possession and Larson tipped in his own missed shot to give the Mustangs their largest lead, 38–30 with 3:27 remaining in the third.

After Brandenburg hit both ends of a two-shot foul, guard Dave Hamstra connected on a jumper in the lane to maintain the eight-point lead with 2:23 left.

But with five seconds remaining in the period Redelman picked up his third foul, sending Jason Lintner to the line for a one-and-bonus. He sank them both, and Kouts' lead was 40–34 as the game entered the final period.

With all the marbles now up for grabs, Rensselaer shook off the lethargy of the third period. Thirty-seven seconds into the fourth quarter Brandenburg slammed home a two-handed jam. Twenty-six seconds later Obermeyer picked up his fourth foul trying to stop Gehring going strong to the hole. He did stop him, but Gehring went to the line and sank the two free throws. Obermeyer went to the bench and sat down. Rensselaer was within two, 40–38.

For the next three and a half minutes, the amount of time Obermeyer was on the bench, the Bombers outscored Kouts 9–7, tying the score at 47 with a jumper from the left side by Brandon Cain with 3:39 left in the game.

In the final three minutes the game was tied four times. With the Mustangs down 51–50 with 2:07 remaining, Redelman stepped to the free-throw line and sank two free throws to put the Mustangs ahead 52–51.

On Rensselaer's next possession Cain attempted a shot from the right corner, it missed, rebounding long. Cain and Kouts' Les Pullins dove for the rebound and collided. Pullins was charged with a foul. That sent Gaff off the bench in a hurry, arguing and pleading with the ref, claiming that Cain had pushed off. But the ref didn't buy it. Cain stepped to the free-throw line and hit both ends of the one-and-one. 53–52, Bombers.

Redelman missed a shot and Rensselaer rebounded. Hooker fired one up, missed, but Gehring boxed out Obermeyer and tipped in the missed Hooker shot. The Bombers led 55–52 with fifty-seven seconds left in the game. Kouts called time-out.

When play resumed, Obermeyer missed a three-pointer. The Bombers rebounded and came downcourt where Swan was fouled. He went to the line for the one-and-bonus, but missed the front end. Obermeyer rebounded and the Mustangs raced down to their end. But Hamstra was fouled. He went to the line for a one-and-one and connected them both, drawing Kouts to within one, 55–54 with exactly thirty seconds left in the game.

On the inbounds play Kouts applied full-court pressure, but the Bombers managed to get the ball in play. Kouts quickly fouled, and once more Swan stepped to the line for the one-and-bonus. He hit them both and again Rensselaer was up three, 57–54 with twenty-seven seconds left.

Kouts broke the Bombers' full-court pressure on the inbounds play, but Redelman was fouled. He stepped to the charity stripe for a one-and-one and an opportunity to bring the Mustangs to within one. He sank the first, but the second one lipped off and Rensselaer rebounded. The score was 57–55 with thirteen seconds remaining.

Kouts quickly fouled, sending Gehring to the line for a one-and-one. He missed. Kouts rebounded, and raced down the floor. Eleven seconds remained.

"I thought about calling my last time-out then," said coach Gaff afterwards, "but with the trouble we had fighting their press, I didn't want to give them time to set up a defense against us, so I just let it ride."

The ball was swung over to Obermeyer who attempted an NBA-range three-pointer with five seconds showing. It clanged off the rim, but Larson raced in to grab the rebound, his legs kicking out wide. He put the ball on the floor, then went up with it, but it, too, missed the mark. Rensselaer took the rebound and the gun sounded. 57–55. Rensselaer.

The Rensselaer fans stormed the floor, piling on one another. A Rensselaer cheerleader was shaken up, but recovered. The Mustangs walked quietly to their dressing rooms. Some of their fans cried.

Larson was the leading scorer for Kouts with 14 points. Obermeyer finished with 13 points and 12 rebounds. McNeil finished with 11 points. Redelman, who played well defensively, shot poorly from the field. He was one of nine from the floor and four of six from the free-throw line for a total of six points.

Rensselaer placed three in double figures. Leading the way was Gehring with 15 points and 12 boards, Brandenburg with 13, and Swan with 11.

"We had our chances," said Gaff outside the dressing room. He had spent ten to fifteen minutes with his players before coming out. "Sam pulled up for the last shot, and it was a good one. I can't argue with him there. He probably didn't know he had more time, but it was a good shot under the circumstances.

"When Sam got his fourth foul that was definitely a key part of the ball game," Gaff continued. "We have had trouble playing without him all year, and it showed here tonight, too."

But Gaff was proud of his team, as well he should be. They finished 17-6 for the season, 30-15 including the 1989-90 season. Kouts also won the 1991 Porter County Conference tournament at Valparaiso.

"They are a great bunch of kids," Gaff said. "They played hard together, and I'm sure gonna miss those seniors. Just a fine group. And, yea, winning the PCC tourney was the highlight, as was the win over Lowell."

Then Marty Gaff, who had just completed his eighth year as head coach, shook hands and disappeared behind the locker-room door.

Evansville Sectional
Evansville Harrison vs. Evansville Bosse
Friday, March 1, 1991

The long-awaited rematch between Bosse and Harrison brought an anxious crowd to Roberts Stadium. The air of anticipation hung heavily over the nervous fans. A sectional championship berth was at stake, and despite the fact that neither of these teams had won the Southern Indiana Athletic Conference, conventional wisdom held that the winner would go on to routinely beat the winner of the Reitz–Central game and claim the championship.

The Evansville Central Bears had won both the conference and the city championship. But Bosse had lost most of their games without Elkins and Darrett, Harrison had gotten off to a shaky start, and Central had been so inconsistent that no one believed Central could play with the real Harrison, or a healthy Bosse. In fact most felt that

Central would probably not get by Reitz, a team of tough, hard-nosed kids from the west side that had given many good teams all they could handle.

This prevailing attitude was dealt a near-death blow when Central manhandled Reitz 79–54. Behind Earl Madison's hot shooting the Bears jumped out to a 15–4 lead and never looked back. Madison admitted to having more than a few butterflies before the game. "I was so nervous at the beginning of the game that I didn't even want to shoot. After I got a couple of layups off fast breaks I got my confidence going."

Joining Madison for game-high-scoring honors was Scott Boyden who also had 11 rebounds. Boyden was another member of the summer's AAU team, and there were those who thought that he didn't belong there. Chosen mostly for his size (6-foot-6 202 pounds) he was not always that impressive as a junior. But according to Central coach Morris Clark the opportunity, and Boyden's hard work, transformed him into one of the best players in Evansville.

As if Bosse and Harrison didn't have enough to worry about in facing each other, they now knew that the winner would have to face a confident and, thanks to their easy win, well-rested Central team.

The marquee game was nothing short of sensational. Bosse guard Antwan Pope was supposed to be that extra player that would make the Bulldogs a great team instead of just a good one. But, as often happens in high school basketball, things didn't go the way they were supposed to. During the season Antwan had never shown the consistency from the outside necessary to free up Bosse's inside game.

When he began the game looking like the player coach Mullan had hoped for all season long, Bosse fans had ample reason to believe this would be their night. Pope scored 8 of Bosse's first 10 points, and played with a confidence that he had lacked during the regular season. A basket by Elkins at the 3:25 mark of the first quarter put Bosse up by three at 12–9.

With Bosse appearing to be clicking on all cylinders, Harrison's Iceman Brent Kell assumed center stage. Kell hit a three-pointer, forced a Bosse turnover, hit another three-pointer, and fed Walter McCarty for a layup all before the Bulldogs could get off a shot. Bosse's lead turned into a 17–12 deficit in less than fifty seconds. After exchanging baskets, the quarter ended with Harrison leading 19–14.

Opening the second quarter Bosse could find no rhythm on offense, and Harrison took advantage. Baskets by McCarty, Darren Winstead, Kevin Hardy, and Kell gave the Warriors their biggest lead at nine. At the 4:22 mark Harrison again went up by nine and were threatening to break the game open, but Bosse's defense held Harrison scoreless the rest of the way. The Bulldogs scored the last nine points despite twice missing the front end of one-and-ones. Brent Kell missed a three-pointer at 0:07 that resulted in a long rebound and a breakaway dunk by Darrett as time expired. The Bosse players went racing to the locker room with a tie score and momentum clearly on their side.

The third quarter saw five lead changes and three ties. Brent Kell continued to be a thorn in Bosse's side hitting 2 three-pointers, both to put Harrison up by a point. In the final quarter Harrison twice threatened to pull away and each time Bosse surged back. After back-to-back turnovers by Bosse and a technical foul on Courtney Dixon for slapping the backboard, Harrison found themselves up 58–51 at the 5:41 mark. But a three-pointer by Darrett and a rebound basket by Elkins made it 58–56.

But Brent Kell would not let Bosse have the lead. He hit the next shot to make it 60–56, and after an Antwan Pope hit cut it back to two at 60–58, Kell drew a foul and hit one-and-the-bonus to make it 62–58.

After a three-point play by McCarty, Darrett hit for three and then for two to make it Harrison 65–Bosse 63 with 3:24 left to play. With Harrison guard Darren Winstead going to the line for two shots Mullan called time-out. Winstead then missed both, and at 2:39 Elkins drove the baseline for a bucket to tie the score at 65, and the Bosse fans exploded.

With just under two minutes Brent Kell—who else but Brent Kell—drove the right side, went up and was clobbered by Elkins who picked up his fourth foul. Kell walked to the line, the referee handed him the ball, and without even taking time to concentrate he let the first one fly. Swish. The second did the same.

With Harrison leading 67–65, Elkins then went to the line for two, and hit one to make it 67–66 at 1:40. At 0:52, Harrison forward Kevin Hardy committed his fifth foul sending Elkins to the line for two. A time-out by Harrison could not ice the Bosse center, and he calmly sank both free throws to give Bosse their first lead since the third quarter 68–67 with just fifty-two seconds remaining.

And then, Bosse lost the game. They lost the game that belonged to them. With nineteen seconds remaining Brent Kell missed his only shot of the final quarter and the rebound fell right into the hands of Bosse's Rohi Fentress. With time running down—17, 16, 15—Fentress threw the ball out to Ron Darrett as the Harrison players scrambled to foul and stop the clock.

Three players swarmed on Darrett, and Darrett went into the air to try to throw a pass over them and back to Fentress. The pass was deflected, and Harrison's Darren Winstead, who was streaking back toward his own basket to help out, saw the ball land right between himself and the basket with Fentress the only Bosse player within ten feet. Winstead picked up the ball and hit a ten-foot jumper over Fentress with thirteen seconds left to give the Warriors the lead at 69–68.

Bosse inbounded the ball and caught Harrison asleep. Andy Elkins got the ball at the top of the key with only one defender between him and the basket. He drove to the right, and Darrett was open for a twelve-foot jumper, but Elkins with his Harrison defender all over him decided to drive the ball to the hoop and try to get the layup or the foul. It was not a bad decision. After all, it was the sort of thing that Elkins had been doing for the Bulldogs all season. The ball flew out of Elkins' hands and there appeared to be plenty of contact. The referee blew the whistle and as all eyes fell upon him, he raised his arm and called the ball out-of-bounds to Bosse with two seconds left. Elkins scowled at the ref, and coach Mullan wanted a time-out to set up the last play.

When Bosse took the floor, Harrison called time-out after they had a chance to look at what Bosse was setting up. When the two teams again took the floor, Bosse could not get the ball inbound and had to use their last time-out. After what seemed like an hour, the teams took the floor. Bosse broke Elkins into the middle and posted him up for a lob pass, but the Harrison defense denied it. With the five seconds nearly up, Elkins had to break down the baseline to take the pass. From the three-point line he turned and launched a desperation shot while falling out-of-bounds. The shot didn't draw iron.

Elkins continued out-of-bounds, grabbed a gate from the barrier that separated the fans from the playing floor, and pulled it off its hinges as the Harrison fans mugged each other at centercourt. The Bosse players did not move from the spots they had occupied when Elkins' shot had come down. They stood perfectly still, and realized that their season was over. They had begun the season as the state's third-ranked team. They had set for themselves the goal of winning the state championship, and now it was over.

Coach Mullan's concern was for his kids. "I can get over it," said Mullan after the game, "My concern is for these seniors who gave it their all. It'll take some time for them to realize that the sun will come up tomorrow."

Brent Kell led all scorers with 27 points, and went 7 for 7 at the line. Bosse's Andy Elkins finished with 23 points and 15 rebounds. Ron Darrett, who will move on to play for Ball State next year, had 18 points including 2 three-pointers in the fourth quarter.

Evansville Harrison vs. Evansville Central
Saturday, March 2, 1991

In the championship game Harrison would play Central. Harrison had knocked themselves out playing Bosse, and Central had proven it was a team that could win the championship by easily whipping Reitz.

The game for the championship may have been even better than Bosse–Harrison. A well-played first quarter saw five ties and four lead changes. Central led 23–21 after guard Mike Cunningham hit a pair of free throws with one second left.

The second started off much like the first until Brent Kell led his team on an 11–2 run to give Harrison a seven-point lead at 36–29. A three-pointer by Cunningham cut the lead to four, and a jumper by guard Billy Calloway with three seconds left in the half cut the lead to three at 40–37.

In the third, the teams exchanged baskets six times, and at the end of the quarter Central still trailed by three at 54–51.

The fourth quarter got under way with a breakaway dunk by Central's Calloway that brought the Bears to within one at 54–53. For the next three minutes the lead kept fluctuating between three points and one. Hardy hit for the Warriors to make it three, Calloway hit one-and-the-bonus for Central, Kell hit for Harrison, Scott Boyden hit for Central, and on it went until nearly the three-minute mark. Leading 60–59, Kell committed a turnover and Mike Cunningham took advantage to give Central their first lead since early in the second quarter.

But it was Kell that got the lead back for Harrison with a pair of free throws at 2:47 to make it 62–61. After Scott Boyden hit the first of a one-plus, Harrison's Kevin Hardy got a rebound bucket at 2:08 to give Harrison a two-point lead 64–62.

Central was able to cut the lead to one at the 1:30 mark, but at 1:07 the Bears sent Brent Kell to the line for a one-plus. The first did draw some iron before going in, but the second was nothing except net, and when Central brought the ball upcourt Harrison led 67–64 with less than a minute to play.

Much like Bosse the night before, it was Harrison's game to lose, and they did. Afer a basket by Central's Calloway cut it to one, Harrison's Brian Spear was sent to the line for a one-and-one with thirty-nine seconds remaining. Spear, you may recall, was the hero of the first Harrison–Bosse game during the regular season. Central coach Morris Clark called time-out as Spear approached the line. Spear missed the front end to give Central a chance to take the lead with less than thirty seconds to play.

But Central turned the ball over and with seventeen seconds left, the Bears were forced to foul Darren Winstead. Winstead, like Spear, missed the front end again giving Central a chance to take the lead. After a missed shot, Harrison fouled Mike Cunningham sending him to the line for a one-and-one with only six seconds left. The score was 67–66 Harrison.

Cunningham missed the front end, but Central's Scott Boyden, the member of the summer's AAU team that had improved so much, pulled down the rebound and went up for a five footer. He missed, but tipped in his own miss with three seconds left. Harrison called time-out at 0:02, but Brent Kell's half-court shot as time expired fell short and the Evansville Central Bears had defied the odds to win the sectional.

After the game, the Central locker room was like Mardi Gras. Scott Boyden, who had hit the winning shot, got the attention of everyone by standing on the bench in front of his locker joking with his teammates. He had hung a large section of the victory net from his ear, and his teammates roared with laughter.

Central coach Morris Clark was happiest for his seniors. ''Everybody said we backed into the city championship, so this feels really great. We got excellent help on defense, especially on Kell, we didn't want to let him beat us. And we had good balanced scoring. Two years ago this team finished the season with only six wins, and last year we only had eight; I'm really proud of how our seniors played.''

Central was led in scoring by Billy Calloway with 25, and by Scott Boyden with 14. Harrison was led by Brent Kell with 23. During the early signing period Brent signed a national letter of intent to play with Niagara. After a great deal of hard work his goal of playing for a Division I school had been accomplished. Also for Harrison 6-foot-9 junior Walter McCarty scored 18.

The season was now over for Harrison and Bosse, considered by most to be the teams with the best chance of making it to Indianapolis. When coach Mullan was asked before the season why the city of Evansville had not fared better on the road to Indianapolis he said, ''If you look at most big cities, none have done much better than Evansville. The competition is so tough here that often the best team doesn't even make it out of the sectional.'' Though it may upset many Central fans to hear it, Mullan's words were prophetic.

12

Regionals

March 9, 1991

The sectionals littered the landscape with some pretty heavy names, like Bedford and Martinsville and Ben Davis.

The No. 2-ranked Stars of Bedford fell to unranked Jennings County (10–11) in the first round of the Seymour sectional. The No. 3 Martinsville Artesians (21–2), only two weeks earlier the top team in the state, lost to unranked Bloomington South (14–7) on their own floor in their own sectional in the first game.

At Seymour, the defending state champs, Bedford, scored only two points in the third quarter as Jennings County rallied to win 50–45. Michael Deaton led Jennings County with 15 points.

At Martinsville, meanwhile, the Bloomington South Panthers avenged a January loss to Martinsville to beat the Artesians 67–58. The Panthers were led by Chris Brand's 20 points and Scott Grissom's 18. Chris Miskel chipped in another 17.

During the regular season, on Friday, January 4, Bedford had beaten Jennings County on the same evening that Martinsville beat Bloomington South. Then on February 9 Bedford beat Martinsville, knocking the Artesians from the No. 1 spot.

Up at the Michigan City sectional, No. 18-ranked Laporte (20–3) knocked off No. 13-ranked Michigan Elston (18–4) 91–74 despite the 27 points from Elston's Charles Macon.

Two unbeaten teams remained alive after the sectional round. No. 5 Washington Catholic (22–0) downed defending sectional champion Loogootee 54–51. Catholic's Brian McAtee scored 17 points and Shane Steimel chipped in another 15 to lead the Cardinals.

At the Fountain Central sectional, Fountain Central (23–0) beat Covington 55–43.

No. 4-ranked Brebeuf, with Alan Henderson, and No. 1-ranked Gary Roosevelt, with Glenn Robinson, breezed through their respective sectional championship games.

Brebeuf pounded defending Ben Davis sectional champ Pike 67–38 behind Henderson's 24 points and 29 rebounds.

Gary Roosevelt, meanwhile, had no trouble with Gary West, beating the Cougars 79–69 in the third meeting of the year between the two teams. Robinson and guard Jeffrey Graham each scored 22 points to lead the Panthers to their second straight sectional title.

Brebeuf, however, barely survived the first round of the sectional against No. 19-ranked Ben Davis. Brebeuf had lost to Ben Davis back in January in the Marion County tournament, the only team to beat Brebeuf in the regular season. When the same two teams drew one another in the sectional, the rematch was eagerly awaited. The rematch didn't disappoint.

A crowd of 5,000 squeezed into the 4,200-seat Giant gym at Ben Davis High School to see the game. At the end of regulation, the score was tied at 53. Henderson fouled out with 31.5 seconds remaining in regulation when he went up for a rebound. Unfortunately for Henderson, he also went up over the back of Ben Davis center Bruce McCain in the process. Henderson finished the evening with 30 points, 10 rebounds, and 6 blocked shots.

But Brebeuf's senior guard Greg Barber and freshman Larry Courtney combined for four free throws in the final twenty-three seconds in overtime to ice the 61–57 victory.

The matchup between the two Mr. Basketball candidates was still on course, although the only way they could meet would be in the championship game at the state finals.

And a lot of teams remained to be confronted before then.

On February 28 it was announced that Glenn Robinson had been named to Parade Magazine's annual high school All-American team. Robinson was one of ten players on the first team.

At East Chicago

When it was over, coach Ron Heflin slipped through the mass of people swarming onto the court, people who were screaming and jumping up and down and slapping high-fives and shouting, "We're number one!" He graciously accepted the congratulations offered by these appreciative and enthusiastic fans and he shook some hands, too, but he didn't stop. He didn't stop to accept the trophy, nor did he stop to witness the traditional net cutting.

He turned right out of the gymnasium and stepped around the sawhorse that bore the sign, "players and coaches only," and walked slowly down the long, almost empty, hallway. A couple of folks there slapped his back and shouted their congratulations, but still he did not stop. He didn't stop, in fact, until he pushed through the door of the Gary Roosevelt locker room. Then he sat down.

He sat down on an empty bench in an empty, quiet locker room; the cheers and shouts from the nearby celebration now inaudible. He patted his yellow silk tie and brushed his hands lightly across the lap of his dark suit. He squeezed his tired eyes with his thumb and forefinger and then, though he had a headache, he smiled.

Days before the East Chicago Regional, folks were already talking about the probable rematch between Gary Roosevelt and Andrean. The two teams had opened their respective seasons against one another back on November 19. And what a game it had been. Overtime, two highly touted players (Brandon Brantley and Glenn Robinson) from opposite teams recruited by the same college (Purdue), a packed Andrean gymnasium, and a deluge of press (print, radio, and television) all coming together to kick off the season. When it was over Gary Roosevelt prevailed 66-60. Brantley ended up with 27 points, while Robinson finished with 24.

The rematch was paved by Andrean winning the Hammond Morton sectional 77-68 over Hammond High, and by Gary Roosevelt easily handling the Gary sectional 79-69 over Gary West. All that remained for the rematch to actually occur was for Andrean to beat Lake Central in the morning game of the East Chicago Regional, and for Gary Roosevelt to knock off East Chicago Central in the afternoon game. Then the two could slug it out for the regional championship that night—on a neutral floor.

Lake Central nudged this scenario a little closer to reality by bowing to Andrean 57–53. Someone, though, forgot to tell the East Chicago Central Cardinals about this plan. But even if informed of it, it is doubtful they would have complied.

For the Cardinals wanted to settle a score. Back on January 18 the Cardinals had traveled to Gary Roosevelt only to suffer a 61–46 thrashing. Now, here was an opportunity to pay back the Panthers and win the regional title at the same time. All on their home court, too.

A sold-out crowd of 8,050 jammed into the John A. Baratto Athletic Center on the afternoon of March 9 to witness No. 1-ranked Gary Roosevelt battle No. 15-ranked East Chicago Central. Even the commissioner of the Indiana High School Athletic Association, Gene Cato, felt it necessary to be there. He sat at midcourt, third row.

Robinson knocked the opening tip to Carlos Floyd, and eleven seconds later Floyd scored the first points of the game. Roosevelt raced out to a 13–6 run in the first four and a half minutes of the game with all starters putting points on the board.

Then the Panthers went cold. In the final 3:15 of the opening quarter East Chicago outscored Roosevelt 10–2 with Robinson's tip-in of his own missed shot providing the sole basket during the Cardinal run. When East Chicago's Robert Battle hit a jumper, his eighth point of the quarter, with only two seconds remaining, the Cardinals owned an 18–15 edge.

East Chicago opened the second quarter with a 5–0 run to put the Cardinals up 23–15 with 6:50 left. The run was capped by Brian Isbell going around Roosevelt's Ryan Harding to tip-in a missed free throw by Cardinal Gregory Airington.

In the next two and a half minutes Roosevelt was only able to score four points, all by Robinson. The Cardinals, meanwhile, rattled off another six, and when Airington sank a soft jumper from the corner to give the Cardinals a ten-point lead, 29–19, with 3:57 left in the half, the predominately East Chicago fans erupted.

The teams traded baskets, and with 1:39 remaining, the Cardinals called time-out. When play resumed East Chicago spread the floor and went into a stall. Roosevelt's Carlos Floyd taunted the Cardinal guards, waving them to come at him, shouting to them to come on. East Chicago's stall worked for about a minute and a half, then Roosevelt forced them into a turnover. Roosevelt capitalized on the error with Floyd hitting a jumper in the lane with four seconds left in the half to bring East Chicago's double-digit lead down to 33–25. The

Cardinal's Gregory Airington attempted a three-point heave at the buzzer, but it only bounced high off the glass.

Roosevelt's eight-point deficit at half wasn't too bad considering they shot only 37 percent from the field. Ten of the Panthers 25 first-half points were from Robinson with Floyd close behind with 8.

East Chicago, on the other hand, had no one in double figures at half, but Battle and Isbell each had eight points and Charles Ricks had nine. The Cardinals were shooting 45 percent from the field.

Roosevelt's Ryan Harding opened the second half scoring with a couple of free throws. Airington answered with a high arching shot from the lane, then Roosevelt's Jeffrey Graham nailed a three-pointer from the left side, his first points of the game, to cut East Chicago's lead 35–30 with 6:18 remaining.

But Charles Ricks stuffed one home on a steal, and after Roosevelt missed on the next possession, Robinson inadvertently tipped in a Battle jumper to help put the Cardinals again up by nine, 39–30, with 4:40 remaining.

On the next possession Floyd connected on a jumper, and ten seconds later Roosevelt called time-out with 4:20 left and behind 39–32.

When play resumed Ricks scored on an easy layup to once again stretch the Cardinal lead out to nine, 41–32. Then the Cardinals went cold. Robinson hit a turnaround jumper, then Floyd ran an easy layup. Robinson scored again on two free throws, then again on another turnaround jumper to bring the Panthers to within 41–40 and their fans to their feet.

East Chicago's Isbell hit an easy one underneath, but Roosevelt's Graham answered with a jumper to keep the Panthers within one, 43–42. Airington then went to the line for a one-and-bonus, hitting both, putting the Cardinals up 45–42 with only 1:11 left in the third quarter.

But Roosevelt's Graham hit a jumper in the lane at the 1:00 mark, and thirty seconds later Robinson slammed home his eighth point of the quarter by jamming the rebound of his own missed shot, shaking the entire basketball standard, as well as the Roosevelt fans, to give the Panthers the lead for the first time since late in the first quarter. The third period ended with Roosevelt on top 46–45.

When any game is on the line, especially a tournament game, you have to go to your money-man at crunch time. In Roosevelt's case that can only mean Mr. Robinson. Robinson opened the fourth quarter with yet another turnaround jumper to stretch the Panther lead to

48–45. But the Cardinals answered with an 8–0 run to regain a 53–48 lead with 6:31 remaining in the game. Robinson then connected on another turnaround jumper in the lane. East Chicago's Ricks replied with one of his own. Robinson then scored two straight turnaround jumpers to bring Roosevelt to within 55–54 with exactly 5:00 minutes left.

East Chicago's Battle scored on a layup, then Ricks sank two free throws to pull the Cardinals out to a 59–54 lead with 4:12 remaining.

Roosevelt brought the ball down the floor, kicked it around outside then lobbed it to, guess, Robinson. Swish, a turnaround jumper. Forty-five seconds later, swish, another turnaround jumper to bring the Panthers back to within one, 59–58 with 3:15 left. East Chicago called time-out.

When play resumed Airington scored on a jumper in the lane. Robinson was fouled on the ensuing play downcourt. He stepped to the line and calmly sank both ends of a one-and-one. Roosevelt was again within one, 61–60 with 2:30 remaining.

Battle drilled a jumper and Roosevelt's Darryl Woods answered by hitting both ends of a one-and-bonus. Then Battle connected with another jumper from the left corner, only for Woods to respond with one of his own to keep Roosevelt on East Chicago's heels 65–64 with only sixty-seven seconds left.

With thirty-eight seconds remaining and the score still 65–64 Roosevelt called time-out. The Cardinals' Airington was going to the line for a one-and-one and Roosevelt wanted to make him think about it. He hit the first, but missed the second. East Chicago 66, Roosevelt 64.

Roosevelt brought the ball down the floor with all 8,050 fans on their feet. East Chicago's Ricks then fouled Ryan Harding, sending him to the line for a one-and-bonus with twenty-six seconds left and a chance to tie the game. The Cardinals called time-out.

When the whistle blew to commence play, Harding stepped to the line and quickly sank the front end. The Roosevelt fans went wild. The ref bounced the ball back to Harding who dribbled it three times, set, fired, and swish. Tie game at 66. The gymnasium was rocking. Twenty-six seconds left.

East Chicago inbounded the ball, broke the Roosevelt press, got the ball to midcourt, and called time-out with nineteen seconds left.

When play resumed, Roosevelt's Jeffrey Graham kicked the ball out-of-bounds on East Chicago's inbounds attempt. Still nineteen seconds to go.

East Chicago's Ricks inbounded to Battle who got it back to Battle who fired from the left side with six seconds left, but the ball bounced out-of-bounds off the fingers of Floyd. Still Cardinal ball. Again Ricks inbounded the ball to Battle, but this time Battle walked. Panther ball. Roosevelt called time-out with three ticks on the clock.

When play resumed Carlos Floyd attempted to put the ball in play, but it was stolen by Airington who quickly tossed it toward the basket. It missed. Overtime.

Robinson began the 3:00 overtime period by tipping the center-jump to Floyd. The Panthers then scored four straight points in the next forty-seven seconds. First, Robinson hit a turnaround jumper, his 34th point of the game. Then Darryl Woods connected on both ends of a one-and-one to give Roosevelt a 70–66 lead with 2:13 remaining.

East Chicago's Maurice Billups then scored his only points of the game when he hit a jumper from the right corner to bring the Cardinals to within 70–68 with exactly 2:00 left.

Floyd scored for Roosevelt and Airington answered for East Chicago with a layup. Graham of Roosevelt then ran a layup of his own to give the Panthers a 74–70 lead with 1:20 left.

With 1:09 remaining Robert Battle broke for a layup and was fouled on the play by Darryl Woods. Battle stepped to the line to make it a three-point play. His free throw clanged off the back of the rim, and Gregory Airington stepped around Ryan Harding and tipped in the errant free throw. That tied the game at 74 with sixty-three seconds remaining, and the noise in the John A. Baratto Athletic Center was thunderous.

Roosevelt inbounded the ball and brought it down the floor. East Chicago, however, stole the ball and quickly started running back the other way, but Roosevelt stole it back in a pileup of players at the Cardinal end of the floor. Roosevelt emerged from the confusion with the ball and brought it back down to their end and called time-out with twenty-four seconds left.

When play resumed Carlos Floyd inbounded to Ryan Harding. Everybody in the building knew who the ball was going to. The Panther guards whipped the ball around the perimeter, until only five seconds remained. Then they lobbed it in to Robinson. It was to be a turnaround jumper. He had already made five in a row. What was one more? He took the ball on the baseline at the right side, turned, jumped with three Cardinals hanging on him, and fired. It bounced off the front of the rim. Double overtime.

This time East Chicago got the tip from jump-center to start the second overtime, and thirty seconds later Battle buried a three-pointer from the right side to put the Cardinals up 77–74.

Down at the other end of the court Robinson kept the Panthers alive with another powerful jam with 2:15 left. East Chicago's Marlon Anderson answered with a jumper, to make it 79–76, East Chicago. Twelve seconds later Robinson fouled Charles Ricks, sending Ricks to the line for a one-and-one with 1:45 left. Ricks made the first, but missed the second. Roosevelt rebounded and was down four, 80–76.

Robinson received a bounce-pass down low on the ensuing possession, but his jumper missed the mark. East Chicago rebounded, broke the Panthers' pressure, and maneuvered the ball to their own end of the court. Roosevelt's Darryl Woods then fouled Maurice Billups who stepped to the line for a one-and-bonus. He missed.

Roosevelt rebounded and raced down the court where Billups fouled Robinson attempting a jumper in the lane. As Billups sat down with his fifth foul, Robinson missed the first free throw, but hit the second. Roosevelt was within three, 80–77, with 1:09 left.

With forty seconds remaining in the second overtime Robinson picked up his fourth foul, sending Airington to the line for a one-and-one. He missed the front end, and Roosevelt rebounded.

Ten seconds later Marlon Anderson fouled out, sending Roosevelt's Graham to the line for a two-shot foul. East Chicago called time-out to make Graham sweat a little.

The heat got to Graham who missed both free throws. Robinson, maneuvering past the East Chicago blockouts, grabbed the rebound and was fouled. He was to shoot a one-and-one. Stepping to the line Robinson was 6 for 7 at the free-throw line for the game. Through the thunder of the fans Robinson sank both. Roosevelt was within one, 80–79, with twenty-eight seconds remaining.

On the ensuing possession East Chicago's Battle was fouled, and he went to the line for the one-and-bonus and the chance to extend the Cardinal's lead by three. Again, thunder rained from the stands. Battle crouched and let it fly, but the ball lipped the rim and Robinson grabbed a big rebound, his 17th of the game. Eighteen seconds remained.

(Mike Thomas)

All-State candidate Ron Darrett slams in 2 points for Evansville Bosse. Darrett scored 18 points in Bosse's end-of-season loss to Evansville Harrison.

Whitko's Steve Nicodemus, the state's third leading scorer and all-conference football and baseball player, talks with Hilliard Gates after winning the Arthur L. Trester Mental Attitude award.

(Mike Thomas)

Evansville Bosse coach Joe Mullen (fourth from left) watches his Bulldogs lose the season opener to nationally ranked Peoria Manual. Bosse played well against an excellent team, and after the game Mullen remarked, "I'm as happy with this team's effort tonight as I can be."

"Iceman" Brent Kell of Evansville Harrison has an urgency to lead and an unshakable court savvy that make him that special player of coaches' dreams.

Andy Elkins of Evansville Bosse looks for an open man at the St. Louis KMOX Shootout. Elkins broke his foot later in the season but still made the Indiana High School All-Star team.

(Mike Thomas)

(Mike Thomas)

On Friday and Saturday evenings Charlie Jenkins transforms WXVW Jeffersonville into *the* voice for area high school basketball. Broadcasting since 1964, Jenkins has been named Sportscaster of the Year four times—in 1978, '82, '85, and '87—and earned a brick in the Indiana Basketball Hall of Fame.

"The little book" and its author David M. Pert. Pert and wife Madelyn have been researching and publishing the *Indiana Basketball Handbook* every year since 1968.

(Mike Thomas)

Brebeuf's Alan Henderson (44) and Terre Haute South's Brian Evans battle for position in the first game of the state finals.

Over 30,000 people flocked to the Hoosier Dome to watch the 1990-91 Championship Game. Some 20,000 additional seats were partitioned off, but officials agree they could also have been sold.

(Mike Thomas)

(Mike Thomas)

Glenn Robinson goes over Brebeuf's
Larry Winters for the block. Robinson's
tough defense set the early tone for
Gary Roosevelt's victory, and he finished
the game with 22 points, 10 rebounds,
3 blocked shots, and 4 steals.

(Mike Thomas)

Alan Henderson snags the ball. In spite of his efforts—14 points, 10 rebounds, 5 blocked shots, and 3 steals—the Brebeuf Braves lost 51-32 in the final game of the 1990-91 season.

Henderson boxes out Jeff Hutz of Terre Haute South for the inside position.

(Mike Thomas)

A disappointed Brebeuf team accepts the runner-up trophy. The Braves ended the season at 26-2, their only other loss back in January at the hands of highly regarded giant killer Indianapolis Ben Davis in the Marion County Tourney.

Purdue-bound Glenn Robinson was named Mr. Basketball on April 8, 1991. He received 68 more votes than runner-up Alan Henderson of Brebeuf Prep.

Steve Nicodemus waits to set up the offense in the first round of the state championship. Whitko lost 83-53, the widest margin of defeat in a Final Four game since 1960.

(Rob Banayote)

From October 15, the first day of practice, till mid-March, boys in high school gyms across Indiana have one thing in mind: to reach the Hoosier Dome in downtown Indianapolis, home of the IHSAA Final Four.

The Gary Roosevelt Panthers, 1991 Boys Basketball State Champions.

(Mike Thomas)

Roosevelt brought the ball quickly up the right side. They swung it left, then came back around. Robinson slid to his left. Again, everyone knew who was going to get the ball.

Robinson received the pass on the baseline on the right side. He didn't put it on the floor, instead he just turned and jumped, again with three Cardinals hanging onto him. This time it went in. Then the poker-faced Robinson did something he had never done during a game. Robinson jumped up with jubilation and shook his fist. Not at East Chicago, but in celebration. Roosevelt 81, East Chicago 80 with three seconds left.

There was still time, though. The Cardinals' Abrian Brown inbounded the ball down to midcourt where East Chicago quickly called time-out. Two seconds remained.

When play resumed Charles Ricks inbounded the ball to Brian Isbell who spun and fired a desperation three-pointer. It missed. The Panther fans swept the floor in celebration.

Now Roosevelt could play Andrean.

It was a stellar performance from Glenn Robinson. The Purdue-bound center scored 41 points (a season high), 31 in the second half, and scored all of Roosevelt's 7 points during the second overtime. He scored 14 of Roosevelt's 20 fourth-quarter points, points that literally kept the Panthers in the game. He was 16 of 23 from the field, or 69.5 percent. In the second half alone he shot 12 of 16, or 75 percent. And if that were not enough, he bagged 17 rebounds and slapped away four shots. Not a bad day's work, eh?

"I'm ready to play some more," Robinson said afterwards. "No, I'm not tired at all."

Five hours later he got his chance.

So, the big rematch was going to happen after all. Radio announcers pointed out that Andrean had a very good chance. Roosevelt would be tired after that long, double-overtime victory. Brandon Brantley would be fresh, Robinson fatigued. No doubt about it, said the announcers, it would be close.

It was never close. Roosevelt took the opening tip, scored eight straight points on four straight Andrean turnovers and never looked back. Oh, Andrean did manage to pull within six, 14–8, with 2:47 left in the first, but that is as close as they got. At the end of the quarter the Panthers led by 14, at the half by 20. There was more excitement generated when Purdue coach Gene Keady walked into the gym to see his two recruits play than was generated by action on the court.

Never did Roosevelt's lead drop below double digits after the first quarter. At one point in the third period, the Panthers simply played keep away for a couple of minutes. Their lead was 26 then, what else were they to do?

When the drubbing ended, an 85–57 final, Carlos Floyd had a career high 33 points and Robinson added another 21. The nets were cut down, the trophy presented, and little kids pestered Robinson and Floyd and others for autographs. The Panthers *owned* the East Chicago Regional.

Heflin looked up after smiling.

"We've got more than one player on this team," he said. "I've been saying that all year. Carlos showed that tonight. So did Jeff and so did Ryan Harding.

"This is a veteran team. I've got nine seniors on this team. They know how to handle big games. I knew, I knew we would not lose against East Chicago. We just had too much experience and talent. And I knew we weren't out of gas after that game. I knew we would come back strong in the night game.

"The difference between the first Andrean game and tonight was just opening-night jitters, that's all. But that was twenty-seven games ago, and as I said, this is a veteran team. Nothing is going to shake it."

He paused. Then he said quietly, "If Glenn isn't the best player in the state of Indiana there is no sun in the universe."

At that moment someone entered the locker room and asked Heflin if he would talk to the radio and TV people. He shook his head no. "Let the kids be in the spotlight," he said. And with that the man who had just won his 297th career victory was left to be by himself in an empty locker room.

Seymour Regional

At 9:45, one hour and fifteen minutes before game time, and fifteen minutes before the doors were to open for the morning sessions, the street outside the Seymour gymnasium was lined with cars. This, and the crowd of about 500 that had already gathered at gates one and two, made for a parade-like atmosphere for arriving fans to display their enthusiasm. Decorated cars rolled down the street with honking horns and screaming girls poking out of sunroofs. Things really got rocking when the Jeffersonville student booster section showed up, and by 9:55 it was so loud that it was nearly impossible to hold a conversation with the person next to you.

Seymour has become a great regional in recent years. It is here that Damon Bailey played three times on his way to the Final Four in Indianapolis, and the one year that he didn't make it his team was taken out by the Floyd Central Highlanders starring Bailey's predecessor as Mr. Basketball, Pat Graham.

This year there were no Mr. Basketball candidates—not for 1991 anyway—but there were two very good teams, one of which would have an excellent chance of making it to Indianapolis. These two teams, Jeff and New Albany, are part of a rivalry that dates back to the infancy of Indiana high school basketball, and remains one of the best in the state.

Back in the good ol' days when New Albany and Jeff were the only heavyweights for miles around, the rivalry was fierce and sometimes savage even off the basketball court. The favorite cheer of the New Albany fans for years has been, "Beat the hell out of Jeff, beat the hell out of Jeff." The Red Devil fans soon countered with "SONA," or Shit On New Albany. Pretty strong stuff for the fans of the '40s and '50s and definitely not in good taste even today.

But this was in a different age of basketball, before consolidation brought other big competitive schools into the picture like Bedford North Lawrence or Jennings County, and also before the creation of Floyd Central in 1968 which took in a large part of what used to be the New Albany district.

In 1991 it is nearly as sweet to beat one of these teams as it is to beat each other. Now the rivalry usually remains on the basketball court where nearly everyone would agree it belongs, but it does make for great storytelling by the old-timers.

For the first time in the long history of Jeff–New Albany matchups this one would be for a regional championship. Both schools have nice gyms that are the largest around, and for years they have fought over who should host the sectional. For a while they alternated, which left neither happy, but last year each was given their own sectional and instead of knocking each other out in the sectional they would do so in the regional. And that is exactly what was to occur tonight assuming Jeff could get by Brownstown, and New Albany could get by Madison.

Brownstown, located about fifteen miles south and west of Seymour, has a population of about 2,500; Jeffersonville has nearly that many in its high school alone. Shortly after the doors opened the Brownstown fans started a cheering contest with the Jeff fans; it was a contest that Brownstown won easily.

Brownstown was a community clearly bursting with pride. The looks on the faces of the fans, especially the adult fans, were like those of a mother whose seven-year-old child was about to give his first violin recital. They were happy and proud just to be here. Some overly optimistic fans were, perhaps, looking for a victory, but most were simply hoping for a good showing so their young representatives could leave with their heads held high.

For a while the optimists were delighted, Brownstown scored the first four points of the game, and at the 2:09 mark of the first quarter the score was tied at 18. After a 10–0 run by Jeff, Todd Isaacs hit a running one-hand three-pointer with one second left to cut the lead to seven going into the second quarter. But Jeff slowly began to pull away. Demonstrating the depth that has made them a Top 20 team, the bench scored 15 of the team's 21 points in the second quarter, and the score at the half was 49–36.

Things only got worse for Brownstown in the second half as Mike Harris and Corey Norman, who is probably the best freshman in the state, took over. Brownstown's Todd Isaacs put forth a herculean effort scoring 34 points, but Jeff put five players in double figures and won the game easily 94–70. The Brownstown fans let their team know how they felt by giving them a bigger ovation than the Jeff fans gave their winning team.

As lopsided as the first game was, the second game was worse. Not only was New Albany bigger than Madison, they were also quicker and stronger. A 17–2 run by New Albany in the second quarter turned this game into a blowout, and the first half ended with New Albany up 47–23. New Albany also had balanced scoring with four players in double figures led by David Brewer with 18 and sophomore Noy Castillo with 14. The final score was 62–40 and the game that everyone had been waiting for was set.

New Albany and Jeff both came into the tournament with very young teams and were generally considered teams of the future. Jeff has four underclassmen averaging in double figures—Joe Estes, Mike Harris, Corey Norman, and Sheron Wilkerson. New Albany has two— Noy Castillo and Pino Pipes—and another, Jay T. Shirer is a starting guard. Because of the upsets of Bedford North Lawrence, Evansville

Bosse, and Evansville Harrison, however, New Albany's chances of making it to the Final Four this year were looking pretty good.

Jeff is a team that relies mostly on its depth, as coach Broughton put it before the game, "We may not have the best starting five, but we have a great starting ten." New Albany relies largely on an excellent inside-outside combination. Six-foot-seven center Pino Pipes provides the muscle inside, and Noy Castillo, Jay T. Shirer, and David Brewer roam the perimeter. Also, the general consensus is that New Albany has one of the best coaches in southern Indiana in Jim Miller.

From the opening tip both teams came out aggressive but not tight. They exchanged baskets at a rapid-fire pace. At the halfway point of the first quarter there had already been four ties and five lead changes. New Albany led at the end of the first quarter 23–21, but the quick pace favored Jeffersonville. Jeff had worn their opponents down in winning 19 of 22 regular season games, and New Albany went no more than 7 deep.

Jeff opened the second quarter with back-to-back baskets by Marcus Pinkston, and then survived five straight missed shots over the next ninety seconds, largely because New Albany turned the ball over three times during that stretch. After New Albany's David Brewer hit a jumper to make the lead 31–29 at the 4:06 mark, Jeff called time-out. Whatever it was that coach Broughton told his team, it worked. Jeff came out and scored nine straight points, held New Albany scoreless for over two minutes, and were threatening to blow the game open. New Albany regrouped in time to stave off disaster and the half ended with Jeff leading 42–37.

Jeff turned up the defense a notch to start the third quarter, holding New Albany to two points through the first five minutes, but Jeff's seven turnovers in the quarter prevented them from blowing away the Bulldogs. By the time New Albany scored their second basket at the 2:57 mark most of the team was looking worn down, and at the 2:35 mark Pino Pipes picked up his fourth foul while reaching on defense instead of moving his feet. Jeff was smelling blood and coach Broughton continued to pull fresh players off the bench.

Opening the fourth quarter New Albany clearly saw it was do-or-die time. At 7:26 Pino Pipes came back in, and the Bulldogs gave it everything they had. Overplaying on defense, they forced back-to-back Jeff turnovers and their fans rocked the gym in support. A three-pointer by David Brewer at 5:59 brought them to within two at 60–58, and Jeff immediately turned the ball over trying to get it inbounds. When Noy Castillo drove the lane for a layup that tied the score at 5:30, the New Albany fans exploded. But on the very next trip down the floor Pino Pipes picked his fifth foul at 5:23 and over the next five minutes New Albany would score only two more points.

Jeff finished the game with a 24–4 run and won going away 84–64. New Albany had played well and given it everything they had, but in the fourth quarter while the Bulldog players were doubled over with their hands on their knees, resting at every opportunity, the Red Devils were substituting in threes.

Jeff was going on to play in the semistate, and win or lose, with the young players they boasted, they would be back even stronger next year. Jeff was led in scoring by junior Mike Harris with 16, and junior Joe Estes with 12. Freshman Corey Norman scored 8 and sophomore Sherron Wilkerson also scored 8.

New Albany was led by David Brewer with 18. Sophomore Noy Castillo scored 14 and junior Pino Pipes had 12.

13

Semistate

March 16, 1991

Perhaps the biggest surprise was Shelbyville. First, the Golden Bears edged Columbus North in the morning game of the Columbus regional. John Heaton, son of coach John Heaton, hit six of six free throws in the last thirty-three seconds to get the win. Then, in the championship game against Bloomington North, non-starter junior Josh Cord rebounded a missed free throw by Chris Dovidas and then hit an eight-foot fall-away jumper with only four ticks on the clock to give Shelbyville the 62–60 win. Shelbyville was the only team to advance to the Sweet Sixteen with a losing record, 11–13.

And how about those Bombers of Rensselaer? A week after winning their first sectional since 1969, Rensselaer won their first-ever regional by slipping past Lafayette Jeff in overtime in the morning game, and then squeaking past Twin Lakes in the championship game.

Lafayette Jeff forced the overtime when point-guard Chip Hammel ran in a layup with five seconds remaining in regulation to tie the game at 85. But junior Bomber guard Jacob Chapman buried a three-pointer with 1:52 remaining in the overtime period to put Rensselaer up for good, 88–85. Chapman then iced the game when he hit one free throw with nine seconds left to give the Bombers the 91–88 victory. That was the first time that Lafayette Jeff had lost a regional game in their home Crawley Center, which opened during the 1969–70 season. Bomber Dan Brandenburg led Rensselaer with 25 points.

In the Twins Lake game, Steve Gehring, the Bombers' center, took a pass from guard Jacob Chapman then fired up an eight-footer at the horn to give Rensselaer a 64–62 win and the regional championship. Gehring led all scorers with 19 points.

Perhaps it was the frustrating loss to Harrison in the sectional, then again, maybe it really was the increased workload forced upon him when he was named head of the physical education department. Whatever the reason, Joe Mullan announced he was stepping down as head coach of the Bosse Bulldogs minutes after his team lost to Harrison in the Evansville sectional.

Mullan's eleven-year reign at Bosse saw him compile an impressive 208–56 record, for a 78.8 percent winning margin. In back-to-back years—1981–82 and 1982–83—his teams went undefeated in the regular season. The 1981–82 team made it to the state finals, but was defeated by Gary Roosevelt in the morning game.

West Lafayette Semistate
Mackey Arena

Purdue coach Gene Keady stood outside the Gary Roosevelt locker room located deep in the bowels of Mackey Arena on the campus of Purdue University. The coach was wearing a white crewneck sweater, the collar of his black shirt sticking out. The coach was also wearing a smile. People passing by him stopped and chatted, wished him luck, and nodded their heads toward the door to the Roosevelt locker room with a knowing grin. In just seven months the young man who was behind that door—the young man who just moments ago had been the one most responsible for qualifying Gary Roosevelt for the state finals down in Indianapolis—would be playing not for Ron Heflin, but for Gene Keady and the Purdue Boilermakers. Mackey Arena would be the young man's new neighborhood. And that was the reason for Gene Keady's smile.

"If we would have had Glenn this year," Keady said, "we wouldn't have lost as many games."

The first hump to cross was Anderson Highland. The Scots were ranked seventeenth and brought to the Lafayette semistate a 22–3 record. Highland's losses had been to Brebeuf, Muncie Central, and Muncie South. Like Roosevelt, Anderson Highland was big on the front line. Six-foot-ten David Foskuhl was in the middle, flanked by 6-foot-7 forward Greg Sager and 6-foot-3 forward Kurt Wilson. Unlike Roosevelt, though, Highland had a pair of guards who could actually put the ball in the hole. Sophomore Randy Zachery averaged 19.3 ppg while fellow sophomore Brad Ash averaged 11.5. Here, then, was a team that could clearly beat Roosevelt. If Highland could at least slow Robinson down with their own formidable front line, yet get good work from their guards, Highland could come out the winner.

Highland took the floor for warmups at exactly 10:40 A.M. Following the team came two students, a boy and a girl, dressed in traditional Scottish garb—plaid kilts, sash, plumed hat, the works. And a la the Anderson Chief and Maiden, the two Scots stood and watched from centercourt as the Highland players went through their warmups.

Exactly two minutes after Highland took the floor, out came Gary Roosevelt. Led by Glenn Robinson, the Panthers circled the court then fell into their warmup routine. The Panther mascot was nowhere to be found. A fan near the court held up a sign that read, "Mackey Arena—Mr. Robinson's New Neighborhood!"

Glenn wasted no time letting people know that this court was *his* territory. Seventeen seconds after the opening tip Robinson finger-rolled in the first points of the game.

Zachery answered with a ten-footer from the left side. Roosevelt's Jeffrey Graham responded with a jumper of his own at the 7:12 mark for a 4–2 Roosevelt lead. But for the next four and a half minutes, the Panthers couldn't find the basket. Meanwhile, Highland's Kurt Wilson buried a 15-foot jumper, Foskuhl nailed a turnaround jumper in the lane, and Zachery connected on another jumper to give the Scots an 8–4 lead with 3:20 left in the first quarter.

Robinson broke the Panthers' dry spell with a turnaround jumper in the lane. But Zachery scored his sixth point of the quarter with a jumper from the right side to give the Scots a 10–6 lead.

Highland then got sloppy. Roosevelt's Carlos Floyd ran back-to-back layups to tie the game at ten with sixty-six seconds remaining in the period. But Highland's Greg Sager scored with only one second showing to give the Scots a 12–10 edge at the end of the first quarter.

For the first three minutes of the second quarter the two teams traded baskets. With the score 18–14 in favor of Highland and with possession of the ball, Jeffrey Graham stole the ball and flipped it to Robinson who jammed it home. Highland inbounded the ball and got it to midcourt, but Robinson stole the ball. He raced downcourt pursued by Zachery. Robinson wanted the slam, but Zachery was able to disrupt Robinson enough so that the big center had to be content with a layup. That tied the score at 18 with 3:57 left. After Highland's Brad Ash's three-point attempt fell short, Roosevelt rebounded, and Ryan Harding fired up his own three-point attempt. It failed, too, but Carlos Floyd rebounded it and put it back up for two. The Panthers were up 20–18, and Highland called time-out with 3:14 remaining in the half.

When play resumed Robinson intercepted a Highland pass, pushed the ball quickly downcourt and stuffed it. On the next possession Zachery drilled a jumper from the right side and was fouled on the play by Graham. Graham sank the free throw, and the three-point play pulled the Scots back within 22–21 with 2:22 left in the first half.

But two quick turnovers by Highland gave Carlos Floyd two easy layups and Roosevelt a 26–21 lead with 1:20 remaining.

In the next fifty-two seconds, though, Highland managed to rattle off six straight points. First, Foskuhl hit a jumper, and on Highland's next possession, he tossed up another one, but Robinson was called for goaltending. Give Foskuhl another two, and the Scots are within 26–25 with forty seconds left. Then with Graham trying to get the ball inside to Robinson, Highland stole the ball and Ash buried a jumper with five seconds remaining apparently to put the Scots up one going into the halftime locker room.

But Roosevelt inbounded quickly, pushed it upcourt even faster, flipped it to Robinson who jumped and swished the nets as the horn sounded. Roosevelt 28, Highland 27.

"Get the ball to Glenn!" Heflin exhorted at halftime. And for good reason. Robinson was six for six from the field, and the Roosevelt guards, as they had been all year, were futile offensively, one of eight. But it was not as though they were not trying to get the ball to Robinson. Of Roosevelt's 8 second-quarter turnovers, 5 were committed trying to force the ball into Robinson. Highland was doing a good job of sagging in on the big man.

And the Scots were shooting better, too. Highland was 13 of 25 in that first half compared to Roosevelt's 14 of 27. Also, all of Highland's starting five had scored. Zachery had 11, Foskuhl 6, Ash and Sager each had 4, and Wilson 2. Roosevelt, on the other hand, got 14 from Floyd, 12 from Robinson, and 2 from Graham. In addition, the Panthers had not gone to the free-throw line one time in the first half. And even though Highland committed eleven turnovers, they were still very much in the game.

The third quarter was a disaster for both teams. Only 10 combined points were scored in the entire period, 6 for Roosevelt and 4 for Highland. The Panthers shot an abysmal 3 of 14, while the Scots shot likewise, 2 for 12. After Robinson hit a turnaround jumper to give Roosevelt a 32–29 lead with 7:10 remaining, no other points were scored for the next four and a half minutes. The Panthers kept trying to push it inside to Robinson, but they either failed or Robinson was unable to connect once he did get the ball. Robinson was two for six in the third quarter.

Finally, the dry spell was broken when Ryan Harding scored his first points of the game with a jumper from the left corner to give Roosevelt a 34–29 lead. But Zachery answered with his own jumper with 1:41 left. The third period ended with Roosevelt on top 34–31.

Forty-one seconds into the final period Roosevelt's Darryl Woods scored his first points of the game with a jumper in the lane. But Zachery responded with a three-pointer from the top of the arc to quickly pull the Scots within 36–34. Harding answered with a field goal.

On the next possession Robinson picked up his fourth foul at the 5:33 mark when he hacked Kurt Wilson. Wilson went to the line for a one-and-bonus, hitting the front end and missing the second. Thirty-three seconds later Wilson slashed through the middle for an easy layup to bring Highland to within one, 38–37 with exactly 5:00 left. Roosevelt called time-out.

When play resumed, Roosevelt's Graham missed a three-point attempt and Highland rebounded. The Scots kept the ball up high on the court, drawing Roosevelt's defense out with them. Then Zachery slipped down low, was fed a pass by Ash, and Zachery layed up an uncontested two points that gave Highland a 39–38 lead with 4:23 remaining in the game. Thirty seconds later Carlos Floyd fouled Zachery sending him to the line for a one-and-one. He sank the first, but missed the second. The Scots now owned a 40–38 lead with 3:58 left.

Roosevelt came up empty on their next possession. Highland took possession of the ball and called time-out with 2:23 remaining.

When play resumed Highland again kept the ball out high, once again drawing Roosevelt's defense out to it, hoping again for a back-door cut. The Scots weaved out high, and suddenly Sager broke free. The ball was snapped to him, and he was all alone underneath. He went up for the easy shot, but from seemingly nowhere came Carlos Floyd and Glenn Robinson, and as Sager jumped for the easy layup, Floyd and Robinson jumped with him. Down crashed the three to the floor, the ball going nowhere near the basket. The Highland fans leapt to their feet screaming foul. Now, such a call against Floyd would have resulted in his third, but such a call against Robinson would have been his fifth. Instead, the ref signaled jump ball. It was Roosevelt's ball, on alternating possession. Alan Darner, the Highland coach, couldn't believe it. He blustered and pleaded with the ref. Boos thundered from the entire arena, except from the area where the Roosevelt fans sat. They cheered. The scoreboard showed 1:44 to play and Highland hanging on to their 40–38 lead.

Roosevelt brought the ball downcourt, tossed it into Robinson who kicked it back out. Again the ball went into Robinson, and this time he spun in the lane, jumped, and let loose. Swish. Tie game at 40 with 1:10 left.

Highland broke Roosevelt's full-court pressure, and as Zachery cut for a layup, Roosevelt's Antonio Lee fouled him before the shot. The layup was no good anyway, and Zachery went to the line for a one-and-one and a chance to put the Scots ahead at least by one. But Roosevelt called time-out to make him think about it. Thirty-six seconds remained.

After the time-out Zachery stepped to the line. He bounced the ball three times, set himself, and shot. Zip. The Highland fans went nuts, Scots 41 Gary 40. Zachery took the ball from the ref once more, bounced it again three times and let it fly. It clanged off the side, and Robinson rebounded, his fourteenth of the game. The Panthers pushed it upcourt, then called time-out with nineteen seconds remaining.

When play resumed Roosevelt's Antonio Lee inbounded to Darryl Woods. The ball was passed around the perimeter, over to Floyd and then back out. Next, it was rifled back into Robinson who had slashed across the lane near the free-throw line. Robinson turned, jumped, and shot. Swish. Roosevelt 42 Highland 41 with :5.3 remaining. Highland screamed for a time-out and got it with :3.4 left.

A stunned Highland crowd and a jubilant Roosevelt crowd stood to watch as Highland's Greg Sager inbounded to Zachery who fired up a three-pointer. It missed. Roosevelt had advanced to the championship game of the semistate.

Of the 14 points Roosevelt managed to score in the second half, Robinson was responsible for 8. He was 10 of 16 for the game. The Panthers shot 41.2 percent for the game, the Scots 41.9. At the free-throw line the Scots were 4 of 9 while Roosevelt was, well, 0 for 0.

"I have never been involved in a game when one team didn't shoot a free throw," said coach Heflin outside the Roosevelt locker room. "I mean, I'm concerned when a team doesn't get to shoot at least *one* free throw. That's gotta be a record. I don't know, I guess Highland didn't foul the entire game." Actually, the Scots committed four fouls. Roosevelt was charged with eleven. But what about that jump-ball call when Floyd and Robinson went up to block Sager's shot? "That's the way the refs called it," Heflin said.

"We should have shot twenty more, 'cause we sure got hacked enough," said an agitated Alan Darner upon being apprised of Heflin's remarks about not shooting a single free throw. "And that jump-ball call. . ." Darner just shook his head. "I thought they traveled a dozen times, they dragged their feet a lot," he continued, "but Robinson is a heck of a player, and he came through when they needed him."

"Things will be different tonight," Heflin said. "They'll get that ball into Glenn, 'cause I'm gonna kick some butt if they don't. That boy scored nearly every time he got the ball. Our guards were shooting too many jumpers. It'll be different tonight."

Roosevelt's opportunity to be different would be against Browns-burg which thumped Rensselaer in the afternoon game 75–54.

A crowd of 12,644 returned for the championship game to see if Brownsburg could pull off the upset. At 24–2 Brownsburg's only losses were to Avon and Center Grove, while the Bulldogs had beaten such formidable teams as Pike and Ben Davis.

Brownsburg was small compared to Roosevelt. The Bulldog's front line was 6-foot-4 center David Wallace, 6-foot-3 Jason Lucas, and 6-foot-2 Shane Headlee. Brownsburg, like Highland in the morning game, hoped to exploit Roosevelt's weak guards while holding Robinson to earthly points.

Heflin's threat to kick some butt must have sunk in, for in the first quarter the Panthers took 17 shots, Glenn shooting 7 of them and making 5. Robinson's first field goal was a jam off a Carlos Floyd steal to put Roosevelt up 6–4. Next, Floyd ran in a layup to tie the score at eight. After an official's time-out at the 3:47 mark, Glenn stuffed another one home off a pass from Jeffery Graham. His next field goal was yet another stuff and thirty-five seconds later he buried a jumper from the left side to give the Panthers a 14–10 lead with 2:02 remaining in the opening period.

Brownsburg's Shane Headlee then connected on a jumper and was fouled on the play by Carlos Floyd. Headlee converted for a three-point play, and Brownsburg was within one, 14–13, with 1:49 to play.

But Roosevelt wound down the quarter with a 6–2 run spurred by Darryl Woods' jumper and a tip-in of Floyd's missed shot. The Panthers finished the period with a 20–15 lead.

Roosevelt quickly stretched their lead out to nine, 24–15, to start the second quarter with layups by Carlos Floyd and Robinson.

But over the next three minutes Brownsburg outscored Roosevelt 10–4 to pull within 28–25. Craig Brunes spearheaded the run with six points, while Robinson kept Roosevelt ahead with a pair of turnaround jumpers in the lane.

After the officials' time-out at the 3:58 mark, however, Roosevelt finished out the quarter with a 10–1 run of their own, with 8 of the 10 points coming from Robinson. Robinson hit a pair of back-to-back turnaround jumpers to stretch the Panther lead to 32–25. After Brownsburg's David Wallace hit the front end of a one-and-one, Roosevelt's Rickie Wedlow hit a jumper with 2:18 remaining to put the Panthers up 34–26. Robinson went to the line for a one-and-one, the first time Roosevelt had gone to the line in the entire semistate; with 1:57 left, he hit the first but missed the second to make the score 35–26.

After Brownsburg failed to score on the following possession, Roosevelt spread the court to take the final shot. The ball was kicked into Glenn who spun and shot with five seconds remaining. The ball rebounded long and was picked up by Wedlow who flipped it to Robinson who was standing behind the three-point arc on the top left side. He fired the three-pointer and it went in as the horn sounded. Roosevelt 38, Brownsburg 26 at half.

Halftime stats showed that Heflin's pleading to get the ball to Robinson was paying off. Robinson had 24 first-half points, including three stuffs, and a three-pointer. He was 11 of 15 from the field and 1 of 2 from the line. He was playing defense, too. He blocked two shots, had two steals, and grabbed nine rebounds. Carlos Floyd was the closest to Robinson with 6 first-half points. All Roosevelt had to do was to hang in there for another sixteen minutes and they were in the Final Four.

After Jason Lucas tipped in his own missed shot to start the second half, the Panthers went on an 8-2 run to go up 46-30 with 5:38 remaining. Robinson started the run with a turnaround jumper in the lane. Lucas connected with a jumper, then Carlos Floyd hit both ends of a two-shot foul. Robinson hit another turnaround jumper in the lane on the next possession, and Ryan Harding completed the run with a jumper from the right side. Brownsburg called time-out.

The time-out cooled off the Panthers. Now Brownsburg went on a run of their own, a 12-4 run. When Lucas buried a jumper near the free-throw line with 2:30 left, Brownsburg had cut the lead down to eight, 50-42. Roosevelt signaled for a time-out, and the Brownsburg fans, who had been quiet, were now back in the game.

When play resumed center David Wallace hit one underneath to cut the Roosevelt lead to six, but Carlos Floyd answered with a layup. Lucas responded with a jumper from the right corner to make it 52-46 with 1:21 left in the third. Eight seconds later Robinson picked up his third foul that sent Wallace to the line for a one-and-one. He hit the first, but missed the second. 52-47.

Roosevelt brought the ball down the floor and Robinson slammed a tomahawk jam and was fouled on the play by Wallace with fifty-four seconds left in the quarter. As Robinson stepped to the line to shoot the extra point, the Brownsburg student section began chanting S-A-T, S-A-T, in reference to Robinson's failure to have passed at that point the NCAA acceptable score on the SAT (Scholastic Aptitude Test). He missed the free throw. But forty-four seconds later he hit another jumper in the lane to give the Panthers a 56-47 lead at the end of three.

Carlos Floyd opened the fourth quarter with his twelfth point of the evening by burying a jumper from the left side with 7:37 showing on the clock. But Roosevelt wouldn't score again for over three minutes. The Bulldogs, meanwhile, would score eight straight points, mostly on free throws.

Headlee began the run with jumper in the lane, then Brunes connected on a twelve-footer to pull Brownsburg to within 58-51 with 6:06 remaining.

Following an official's time-out, Robinson picked up his fourth foul at the 5:33 mark to send Brunes to the line for a one-and-one. He sank both ends. Thirty seconds later Brunes was back at the free-throw line for a two-shot foul. Again he sank both, and the score was now 58–55.

Roosevelt's Antonio Lee broke the ice for the Panthers with a jumper from the left side, but Headlee answered with a pair of free throws to keep Brownsburg within three, 60–57, with 2:42 remaining.

On the next possession Robinson was fouled and sent to the line for the one-and-one. Again the Brownsburg student section cranked up the "S-A-T, S-A-T." Robinson calmly buried both. But ten seconds later Wallace ran in a layup to keep the Bulldogs at Roosevelt's heels at 62–59.

On the next possession Roosevelt's Lee was fouled and went to the line for the one-and-bonus, but Brownsburg called time-out with 1:41 left to make the senior guard think it over.

When play resumed Lee stepped to the line, fired, and missed. Brownsburg rebounded and pushed the ball down the floor where Carlos Floyd promptly fouled Wallace. The Panthers called time-out with 1:22 remaining.

Wallace stepped to the line after the time-out and sank both ends of the two-shot foul. The Bulldogs were now within one, 62–61, and Mackey Arena was rocking.

On the next possession Floyd kicked the ball into Robinson in the low post. Lucas, though, hacked him, and Robinson stepped to the line with fifty-six seconds showing on the clock for the one-and-bonus. The Brownsburg student section chanted its familiar refrain, and Robinson disappointed them by drilling both ends. 64–61, Roosevelt.

Fifteen seconds later Antonio Lee came to the free-throw line after being fouled by Wallace. Lee made both ends of the one-and-one to stretch the Roosevelt lead to 66–61. The Bulldogs inbounded the ball and pushed it to half court, then signaled for time-out with twenty-nine seconds remaining.

But it was all over. Brownsburg never scored again, and Roosevelt's Rickie Wedlow hit two free throws and Carlos Floyd sank another to finish off the Bulldogs 69–61.

"I saw to it that they got the ball to him [Robinson]," Heflin said afterwards in a near-empty locker room. He was sitting quietly with his young daughters on a bench. "He's an exceptional kid. I think he's the top player in the country, and he's definitely the top player in Indiana."

Robinson finished with 36 points, 15 rebounds, 4 blocked shots, and 3 steals. He was 15 of 21 from the field, or 71 percent, and 5 of 8 from the free-throw line. The only other Panther in double figures was Floyd with 13 points to go along with his 8 rebounds.

As a team Roosevelt shot well from the floor, 62 percent, while Brownsburg managed only 46.9. The Bulldogs were also outrebounded 35-21.

Only four of Brownsburg's starting five scored for the Bulldogs. The leading scorer was Brunes with 18, followed by Wallace with 16, Lucas with 14, and Headlee with 13. Lucas led the Bulldogs in rebounding with eight.

"Except for letting them back in the game in the last quarter, we played pretty good," Heflin continued. "But they started standing around, started dribbling off their feet, and trying to dribble through the press instead of passing and that's what got Brownsburg back in it."

"We really wanted this," Robinson said on the court, looking down at the television and radio microphones being thrust up at him. "I thought we played good defense most of the game. Most of the people in the state haven't had a chance to see me play. I hope next week to prove to them what I can do."

For the third time in ten years Roosevelt was going to the Final Four.

Indianapolis Semistate
Hinkle Fieldhouse

An hour before the morning games there were three topics of conversation: the ice storm that had hit just north of Indy, the I.U.-Florida State NCAA Tournament game to be played that night, and the potential matchup between Alan Henderson and Glenn Robinson that could only take place in the championship game in the Hoosier Dome.

The conversations about the ice storm were fairly predictable. Everyone agreed it was terrible, and most had a story to tell from a relative in Frankfort or Kokomo. One man had a sister and a brother-in-law that couldn't get out of their driveway to buy a kerosene heater and went without heat for almost two days.

They were all nearly unanimous in their opinions on the I.U. game as well—Florida State's inside game would give Indiana trouble, but no one really expected the Hoosiers to lose.

The really interesting conversations were over Glenn and Alan as they were known among the fans. Despite the fact that the discussion was being held in the heart of Indianapolis where Alan Henderson had reigned since his freshman year, the locals were about equally divided on who was the better player, and sometimes the debate even grew a little heated. A man in a red sweater insisted that Robinson was the superior player because of his strength and his willingness to bang inside. A man in a red and white sweater countered by saying, "The only reason you think Robinson is better is that you've seen Henderson play, and you've seen that he's human. You've seen him turn it over or go 6 for 20, but the only thing you ever see about Robinson are his points and rebounds in the paper. You never see it when he throws it away or walks or something."

This of course was kind of like saying "you don't know what you're talking about," and the man in the red sweater responded in kind.

"You're crazy, I've seen Robinson play before."

"Yeah, where?" said red and white.

"On TV," responded red.

"How many times?"

"Twice."

A man in a red shirt decided it was time to play peacemaker and jumped in with, "Well, I think you can go on arguing about it forever because I don't think they're ever going to play each other, I don't think Brebeuf can get by Mt. Vernon."

Of course, neither of the men really wanted to pursue an argument and both eagerly followed up on the change of subject. The man in the red sweater went first:

"Yeah, you might be right, I really like Mt. Vernon's balance, and those two big guys might be able to slow Alan down."

The man in red and white wasn't far behind. "They might at least keep him from dominating."

"Exactly, and if he can win the game for them, they don't have anybody else that can," responded the man in the red sweater, and the conversation moved on from there.

The two big men they were talking about were 6-foot-11 junior Brian Gilpin who had already committed to Indiana, and 6-foot-8 senior Chad Kleine who was headed to Bradley next year. Many had yet to see Gilpin play and he was still a bit of a mystery man among the crowd; a lanky, hardworking kid, no one doubted his ability to intimidate on the defensive end, but he often looked lost and clumsy on offense and everybody wondered how it was that he was able to commit to I.U. as a junior.

"I heard he was projected to get up to 7-foot-3," said one woman.

"Well, you can't coach size, and we definitely need that," the man next to her chipped in.

Chad Kleine came into the game averaging 19.3 ppg, and had been the go-to guy for the Marauders all year. At 6-foot-8 he had range out to the three-point line, but he wasn't afraid to mix it up inside either. As anyone witnessing his introduction before the game could tell you, he was clearly a crowd favorite.

Brebeuf was to play Shelbyville in the first of the morning games, and Mt. Vernon was to play Richmond. It should be obvious by now that no one doubted that Brebeuf and Mt. Vernon would be playing that night for the right to go to the Final Four. Shelbyville had come to the semistate as the only team left in the tournament with a losing record (11–13), and few knew anything about them.

"You know anything about Shelbyville?" asked one sportswriter of another.

"Only that they gotta feel lucky to even be here," he answered jokingly. A small conference of writers got together and came up with a little information that would help when they went to write their stories. Shelbyville had gotten off to a 1–8 start mostly because their two best players, 6-foot-3 center Brent Willoughby, and outside shooting specialist Chris Dovidas, had missed much of the early part of the season. No one was really sure why. "Injuries I think," somebody said. Although they finished by winning 8 of their last 11, everyone agreed they couldn't beat Brebeuf.

As for Richmond, they had come through the tough North Central Conference and had beaten Mt. Vernon last year in the semistate, but Mt. Vernon had nearly everyone back from that team and Richmond had lost to some questionable teams. The only problem Richmond was thought to give the Marauders was the press.

"Our press is really devastating. It may be the best press in the state," said Richmond coach George Griffith before the game.

Richmond's racehorse style went far beyond a press. Coach Griffith went on to say, "We try to shoot 80 shots a night and force 25 turnovers. We're not a good jump-shooting team so our best defense is our offense."

Things went pretty much as expected in the first game; Brebeuf jumped out to a quick 6–0 lead and Shelbyville center Brent Willoughby was completely ineffective inside against Henderson. The pace of the game was slow and Henderson was little needed except to intimidate inside. The Golden Bears' Chris Dovidas kept his team close by hitting a three-pointer and scoring 7 of his team's 11 points in the first quarter, but it was obvious that Shelbyville could not win the game as long as Henderson was on the floor.

The second and third quarters went much like the first with Brebeuf steadily building the lead, and after the third the Braves were ahead 38–26. In the opening seconds of the fourth quarter, however, things got interesting. Henderson and Shelbyville's Brian Asher went scrambling for a loose ball. Asher apparently landed on Henderson's thigh and while Asher bounced back up, Henderson stayed down. Things got interesting at that point for two reasons. First it was obvious that Henderson would have to leave the game, and second because the Shelbyville fans started cheering while Henderson was still down.

The opposing fans got into it a bit with each other and began going back and forth with negative cheers. With the crowd back to life and the new uncertainty of Brebeuf's lead, the atmosphere was much more like a typical semistate. Brebeuf held tough at first with their star in the locker room and actually extended their lead to 42–26 on back-to-back baskets by Larry Winters and freshman Larry Courtney.

Leading 44–30, Brebeuf spread the court with 5:25 remaining. At that point Shelbyville went on an 11–3 run getting a three from Travis Heaton and four points from Chris Dovidas. After the Golden Bears forced back-to-back turnovers, converting on both, Brebeuf called time-out at 2:48 with a very shaky 47–41 lead. Henderson came out of the locker room with a heavily bandaged right thigh, and when the Braves took the floor after the time-out he was with them.

Henderson did not score a point the rest of the game, but with his presence, his team outscored Shelbyville the rest of the way 9–6, and won the game 56–46. Henderson finished the game with only nine points, but as the last 2:48 shows, he contributes in a multitude of ways. Chris Dovidas led all scorers with 23 and Larry Winters led Brebeuf with 14.

The second game began with some of the same mean-spiritedness that marred the first game. Although Richmond had come into the semistate a decided underdog, their fans—at least those in the student section—were confident to the point of cockiness. When the Mt. Vernon players took the floor they had to pass right in front of Richmond's student section, and they were subjected to some pretty serious verbal abuse. Although most of it was somewhat good-natured such as, "You should've stayed in Mt. Vernon!" or "You're goin' down!" a small group of rowdier fans hurled obscenities, and one of them kept screaming at the top of his lungs as the 6-foot-11 Brian Gilpin went by: "Get out of here you freak!" The Richmond fans and the Mt. Vernon fans then got into it much the same way the Brebeuf and Shelbyville fans had.

From the opening tip—which went to Richmond despite Gilpin jumping center—it was clear the Richmond fans had plenty to be confident about. After scoring almost immediately and drawing a foul on Gilpin for a three-point play, coach Griffith's Red Devils opened in a press that overwhelmed the much slower Marauders forcing two turnovers in the first fifty seconds.

Richmond looked as if they were going to turn it into a blowout from the word go. The Mt. Vernon players looked shell-shocked as every pass was contested and usually deflected. Guards Roger Huffman and Alex Schank struggled to bring some kind of order to the offense. Two minutes into the game Huffman caught one of the Richmond players overplaying Kleine on defense and hit the 6-foot-8 forward with a pass that allowed him to turn to the basket for an uncontested two points.

The Mt. Vernon team raced to the other end of the floor with broad smiles on their faces, exchanging high-fives when they got the chance. This boost of confidence may have been the most important moment of the game for the Marauders.

A basket by reserve forward Chris White at the 4:54 mark of the first quarter pulled his team to within one at 10–11, but Richmond then went on a 7–0 run with two baskets by Brad Wright and a three-pointer by Billy Wright, and the Red Devils had their biggest lead of the game at 18–10.

Mt. Vernon never really challenged that lead in the second quarter, but they were able to play even with their quicker opponents and keep the game within reach thanks largely to the play of Gilpin. Less than a minute after missing a layup that he was able to place just inches from the rim, he quieted the jeering Richmond fans with a thunderous dunk that brought his team to within 5 at 27–35. He finished the half with a three-point play at the 0:38 mark that cut the lead to 32–35. Trotting off the floor again in front of the Richmond fans there was more jeering, but none directed at Gilpin.

In the third, Richmond turned up the intensity on the press, and after Rod Frazier hit a jumper, Mt. Vernon immediately turned the ball over and Robert Sanders scored to take the lead back up to seven at 39–32. It was about this time that Mt. Vernon defied conventional wisdom and tried something a little different. Instead of trying to pass the ball over or around the press, they simply gave it to 5-foot-8 Roger Huffman and let him try to dribble through it. Huffman did a magnificent job, and in the last seven minutes of the third quarter the Marauders turned the ball over only once.

A 6–0 run by Mt. Vernon on baskets by Gilpin, forward Kevin Browning, and Kleine cut the lead to one at 38–39, and from that point on both teams went on to play some terrific basketball. It seemed neither team could miss as they exchanged basket after basket, and each score seemed more spectacular than the one before. A rebound basket by Gilpin at 3:42 and a jumper by Kleine at 2:38 gave Mt. Vernon their first lead of the game at 44–43. Neither team could build more than a two-point lead and a dunk by Gilpin at 0:25 sent the game into the fourth quarter tied at 51.

Mt. Vernon had given their all to tie the score, but the Richmond coach was taking advantage of his team's depth by substituting his players three at a time, and everyone in the fieldhouse wondered just what Mt. Vernon could have left to give in the fourth.

In the opening seconds Gilpin missed a layup that would have given his team the lead. Richmond jumped out to a four-point lead on two quick baskets by Robert Sanders, and it looked like the Red Devils might be off to the races. Richmond went on to hit seven field goals before Mt. Vernon hit their first at 3:39, but the Marauders were able to stay in the game with uncanny free-throw shooting. After Kevin Browning hit two of two, Roger Huffman connected for one-and-the-bonus three consecutive times at 5:52, 5:34, and 4:17. At the 2:50 mark when Kleine converted yet another bonus opportunity Mt. Vernon was only down 63–68.

Back-to-back baskets by Browning and Kleine then made it 67–68, and after exchanging baskets, Gilpin was fouled and went to the line for one-plus and the opportunity to give his team their first lead of the quarter at the 1:38 mark. Not known for his free-throw shooting prowess, the big center calmly sank one and then the other to take a 71–70 lead.

Richmond's Rod Frazier brought the ball up the floor, and without hesitation pulled up and drilled a three to make it 73–71, and the crowd erupted. With the gym so loud that it was impossible for the players to communicate except by hand signals, Roger Huffman brought the ball up the court against a Richmond press doubled in intensity. Trapped just across the ten-second line, Huffman lobbed the ball to Gilpin where he was fouled with fifty-seven seconds left and his team trailing by two. Richmond called time-out as Gilpin approached the line. After hitting the first to make it 13 straight for Mt. Vernon from the line, the second one spun out and Richmond got the ball back leading 73–72. But while trying to drive the ball inside Richmond turned the ball over and the Marauders went to their go-to guy, Chad Kleine. Kleine got the ball inside and banked in a short jumper at 0:33 to put his team up to stay at 74–73. After Richmond failed to score on their end it was again Kleine who got the ball and the Red Devils were forced to foul with ten seconds left. Kleine failed to ice the game hitting only one of two leaving the door open for a tie or a dramatic last-second three-pointer, but with three seconds remaining Roger Huffman forced a turnover and evaded the Richmond players trying to foul him.

The Mt. Vernon team, cheerleaders, fans, and even the local sportswriter poured onto the court. Brian Gilpin stood a head taller than the crowd that had flocked to center court, and he and Chad Kleine were immediately grabbed for interviews.

The Richmond players and their fans looked on in disbelief. They had the game won and let it slip away. Richmond was led in scoring by Rod Frazier with 20 points and Robert Sanders with 16, both of whom were named to the all-tournament team. For Mt. Vernon, Kleine led the way with 25 on 10 of 15 shooting, and Gilpin had 17 points and 5 blocked shots.

Unfortunately, what should have been a terrific championship game was not. Mt. Vernon, exhausted from the thirty-two minutes of hell-defense that Richmond threw at them, was simply not up to playing a team led by the likes of Alan Henderson.

The Marauders, however, did an excellent job of limiting Henderson's effectiveness. Opening in a 1-3-1 zone, coach Jimmie Howell placed guard Roger Huffman out top, 6-foot-8 Chad Kleine in the middle, and 6-foot-11 Brian Gilpin under the basket. The idea was that whenever Henderson went inside to post up, Kleine and Gilpin would pin him in—Kleine between Henderson and the ball, and Gilpin between Henderson and the basket.

The strategy worked very well in the first quarter limiting Henderson to only a rebound basket at the 1:32 mark. But time after time Mt. Vernon turned the ball over. They turned the ball over against Brebeuf almost as many times as they had against Richmond, and the Brebeuf guards made them pay. Hostetter and Barber accounted for 12 of the team's 24 first-half points.

At the half the Marauders were down only 24–20, but they had scrapped for every point while Brebeuf had missed several opportunities to blow the game open. Henderson had only four points and everyone knew that if he was needed, he could get twice that in the blink of an eye.

Mike Miller's Brebeuf Braves opened the third quarter by going on a 10–0 run to extend the lead to 34–20 at the 4:52 mark. Brian Gilpin broke the run twenty seconds later with a layup, but the Braves then went on another run, this time 6–0 to open a nearly insurmountable 18-point lead 40–22.

Brebeuf coasted in the last quarter and went on to win 73–58. Brebeuf was led by Henderson who scored 14 of his 18 points in the second half, and David Roberts who scored 13. Mt. Vernon was led by Kleine with 13, and Alex Schank with 11 including 3 three-pointers.

Henderson, Brad Hostetter, and Larry Winters made the all-tournament team for Brebeuf. Also on the team were Kleine and Gilpin for Mt. Vernon, Robert Sanders and Rod Frazier for Richmond, and Chris Dovidas for Shelbyville.

Alan Henderson had led his team to the Final Four in the Hoosier Dome. A team that, in the preseason, was not given a chance to make it out of their own sectional. Henderson and company would play Terre Haute South in the morning game. If they could get by South, and Roosevelt could get by Whitko, the dream game between the two best basketball players in the state, and possibly in the country, would be set.

14

State Finals

March 23, 1991

Louis "Bo" Mallard sat at Rick's Cafe American in Union Station in Indianapolis. The place was packed and loud. Mallard was sitting with three members of his family waiting patiently for his lunch to arrive. But he didn't mind the wait, for it allowed him time to savor the game he had just witnessed down the street in the Hoosier Dome.

Mallard had just witnessed the Gary Roosevelt Panthers whip Whitko for the right to advance to the championship game of the state finals, and in the process he had seen his nephew, coach Ron Heflin, win his 300th career victory.

For the second time in ten years Gary Roosevelt would be in the championship game. In 1987 the Panthers earned a berth to the Final Four, but were beaten in the afternoon game by Richmond 66–60. In 1982 Gary Roosevelt managed to climb to the championship game, but ran into a buzz saw named Scott Skiles of the Plymouth Pilgrims. The Panthers lost 75–74 in double overtime. Now Gary Roosevelt was back in the championship game once more, and Mallard was basking in the glow of victory.

Of the four teams that made it to Indianapolis that day—Brebeuf, Terre Haute South, Whitko, and Roosevelt—only one was a former state champion. Gary Roosevelt won all the marbles back in 1968 at Hinkle Fieldhouse, beating Indianapolis Shortridge 68–60 behind the 28 points of Aaron Smith. The head coach of that Gary Roosevelt team was Louis "Bo" Mallard. And helping out Mallard in coaching duties, although not officially listed as an assistant coach, was a tall, skinny guy named Ron Heflin.

Saturday, March 23 was a warm, but very windy day. The sun shined intermittently.

Hoosier Hysteria was even more hysterical than usual, for in addition to the state finals, Indianapolis was about to host the NCAA Final Four as well. Just one week after the state finals the college boys would be coming to town to strut their stuff. On street poles all over downtown were colorful banners reading NCAA Final Four and Welcome to the Final Four. Across the street from the Hoosier Dome, where the NCAA games would be played, was the NCAA headquarters that featured a large hall filled with banners, trophies, and other memorabilia that captured the history of the NCAA Tournament. Even the street running in front of the dome, Georgia Street, had been renamed Final Four Road.

The Embassy Suites Hotel was the headquarters for most of the teams, officials, and fans of the state finals, and the downtown area took on a festive air. Students and their parents strolled the streets (and fought the wind) and packed the downtown restaurants. Union Station—once a train station and now a modern-day bazaar of restaurants, shops, and boutiques—was choked with people. The glass elevators inside the atrium of the Embassy Suites were kept in perpetual motion by students riding them up and down, up and down.

Most of the scuttlebutt the week prior to the state finals was the possible matchup between Henderson of Brebeuf and Robinson of Gary Roosevelt. Last year it had been the near mythic "Damon Bailey game" for the state championship, now a "dream match" between two highly touted players was shaping up. Wow, what a game that would be. The only two candidates for Mr. Basketball going head-to-head, both big centers. One bound for Keady's Boilers, the other for Knight's Hoosiers. Both first-team All-Americans, both the leaders of senior-dominated teams. Mouths were watering at the mere thought. But first there was a little matter of Whitko and Terre Haute South. Remember them?

The first game of the morning pitted Brebeuf (26–1), the smallest of the four schools with an enrollment of 613, against Terre Haute South (23–3). The Braves of Brebeuf were ranked fourth in the final Associated Press poll and were led by Mr. Basketball candidate and I.U.-bound Alan Henderson. The 6-foot-9 200-pound senior center was averaging 27.9 ppg, 14.9 rpg, and 5.1 blocks per game. Brebeuf's only blemish was a 61–53 loss to highly regarded giant killer Indianapolis Ben Davis in the Marion County Tourney back in January. Ben Davis had also beaten Terre Haute South 91–56 back in January.

The three defeats of Terre Haute South had been to Bedford North Lawrence, Ben Davis, and Evansville Bosse. Terre Haute South, also nicknamed the Braves, was led by 6-foot-8 200-pound senior Brian Evans. The I.U.-bound center was averaging 22.2 ppg.

Terre Haute South had made their way to Indianapolis by beating Northview in the sectional, White River Valley in the regional, and Vincennes Lincoln in the Evansville semistate. Terre Haute South's average margin of victory during the tournament was 14.3 points.

At 11:00 country music-star Janie Fricke, once a cheerleader at South Whitley (one of the schools that consolidated to form Whitko), stepped out onto the court. Decked out in a brown jumpsuit and sporting earrings that fell nearly to her shoulders, Fricke sang "God Bless America" and "Back Home Again in Indiana." After Fricke waved good-bye to the crowd of 30,000, Columbus North High School student Carmen Rae sang the national anthem. Then it was time to play basketball. Henderson and Evans stepped into the jump circle, and the tip went to Brebeuf. Thirty-nine seconds later Henderson took a pass from Larry Winters and laid it in for two. Down at the other end Jeff Hutz took a feed from Evan Mills to put Terre Haute South on the board.

The score remained tied for nearly the next two minutes, then Brebeuf's Winters banked in a six-footer on an assist from David Roberts with 5:13 remaining. Brebeuf then went cold, not scoring another point for over three minutes.

Terre Haute South's Jeff Hutz was fouled by Winters who went to the stripe for a two-shot foul. He made the first, but missed the second. Then with 3:13 remaining in the period South's Toby Stephens got a nice feed from Jeremy Harrold and Stephens laid it up for an easy two to give South their first lead at 5–4.

Following an official's time-out at the 2:38 mark, Brebeuf finally broke their dry spell when Hostetter stole the ball and ran the length of the floor for a layup. Again that would be the last time Brebeuf would score for over two minutes.

Evans again put South on top 7–6 when he rebounded his own missed shot and laid it in. Then Evan Mills laid in an easy one with a drive from the right side with fifty seconds left in the quarter to give South a 9–6 lead.

But Winters was fouled on the baseline by Mills with one second showing. Winters stepped to the line for the two-shot foul, missed the first and hit the second to close the opening period at 9–7.

If the first quarter was slow, the second was nearly moribund. Terre Haute South managed only three points that quarter, and that was a three-pointer from Mills on the left side at the 5:40 mark. South did not go to the line during the period and shot one of eight from the field.

Brebeuf, meanwhile, tied the game at nine when Henderson rebounded his own missed shot and laid it back in. Nearly a minute later Henderson stole the ball from Evans and went coast-to-coast for a layup. Fifty seconds later Mills hit his trey to put South back up 12–11.

For the next two minutes both teams went dry. Then Brebeuf got the ball into Henderson who drove left to the baseline, drawing with him South's collapsing 3-2 zone. Larry Courtney then cut to the middle, and Henderson fed him a deft pass for a layup at the 2:40 mark. On Brebeuf's next possession David Roberts tipped in a Greg Barber missed shot to make the score 15–12 at the 2:06 mark, and that was the final scoring for the first half.

The low scoring didn't sit well with some fans, although the Brebeuf fans were probably pleased with being on top, no matter what the score.

But this was the game Brebeuf liked to play. Not having great guards, Brebeuf liked to play the slower, half-court game. And it was working. Not only was Brebeuf on top, but all 13 of Brebeuf's 15 points came from the front line, just as expected. Henderson had 6 points, 10 boards, and a steal.

Both teams increased the pressure to open the quarter. Forty-one seconds into the second half Brebeuf's David Roberts broke from that pressure for a layup, but missed. Henderson rebounded, but was hacked by Jeremy Harrold. Henderson went to the line for a two-shot foul, missed the first, but connected on the second. Brebeuf 16–12.

Terre Haute South pulled within one when Hutz, taking a pass from Harrold, drove to the right side, beating Henderson, and laid it in. Henderson fouled on the play, sending Hutz to the line for the three-point play. Hutz hit, and South was within one at 16–15 with 6:50 remaining in the third.

For the next three and a half minutes the teams traded baskets, and Brebeuf started to full-court press. Then with Brebeuf leading 23–21 with 3:21 remaining, Brebeuf went on a 9–5 run.

Henderson started the run with a layup off a feed from Winters. Then Henderson nailed a 19-footer from a bounce pass from Hostetter to go up 27–21 at the 2:32 mark.

After an official's time-out Brian Evans buried a three-pointer from just right of the key. But Henderson responded with another layup dished off by Winters at the 1:02 mark. Forty seconds later Winters scored on a layup and was fouled on the play by Stephens. Winters converted the free throw, and Brebeuf enjoyed the largest lead of the game, eight points, 32–24.

But Evans closed out the quarter with a pair of free throws when Winters fouled him near the three-point line. The score at the end of three was Brebeuf 32, South 26.

Terre Haute South inbounded to begin the final period, but Evans was promptly called for steps. Three seconds later Evans compounded his error by fouling Henderson. Fortunately for South, Henderson missed the front end of the one-and-one. Hutz got things going for South with a layup from a nice feed from Evans to pull within four, 32–28.

But Brebeuf rattled off four straight points, all on free throws, two by Henderson and two by Hostetter, to give Brebeuf an eight-point lead, 36–28.

South then went on a tear of their own, a 10–5 run over the next three and a half minutes. Hutz started the run with three straight free throws on fouls by Hostetter and Roberts to make the score 36–31. After Brebeuf's Courtney hit both ends of a one-and-bonus, Hutz swooped a hook shot in over Henderson to bring South to within 38–33 with 5:19 left. Brebeuf called time-out.

When play resumed Henderson nailed a three-pointer from the right corner. But South's Mills responded with a three-pointer of his own from the top of the arc, and forty seconds later Evans laid back in a Stephens miss to pull South to within three, 41–38, with 3:32 remaining in the game.

But that would be all for Terre Haute South. They would not score again until 19.4 seconds remained in the game, and by that time it was too little too late, the front end of a two-shot foul by Hutz.

Brebeuf, then, finished the game on an 11–1 run, eight of which were scored at the free-throw line. When the horn sounded it was 52–39, Brebeuf. The Braves were in the championship game, the first time for a private school. Brebeuf had kept up their end to ensure the "dream match" would be played that night.

Henderson finished the game with 26 points, 23 rebounds, 3 blocked shots, and 1 steal. The only other Brebeuf player in double figures was Larry Winters with 10.

The combined 91 points was the lowest point total for a state finals game since 1975 when Loogootee beat Columbus North 50–27 in the afternoon game at Market Square Arena. Henderson's 23 rebounds was the fourth best single-game rebound total in the state finals, behind only Brad Miley (29), George McGinnis (27), and Jim Ligon (24).

"Defensively we did a nice job," said Brebeuf coach Mike Miller, seated at the raised table in the press room. "We created a slow tempo on offense. We couldn't beat 'em in a shooting contest, so we wouldn't let 'em do it. To get them out of sync, that was the best way for us to win, and defense is the way to do it.

"Defense is heart," Miller continued. "A lot of people have underrated the heart of this team, but I think it showed here today. I thought Winters and Roberts did a good job on (Brian) Evans. (Jeff) Hutz hurt us, but it was a trade-off with Evans.

"I thought Alan (Henderson) had trouble with his wind (after last week's injury in the Indianapolis semistate). He didn't practice or go hard all week, and I think he found out you can lose your conditioning pretty quickly. Because of that he did some things out there he normally wouldn't do, but to his credit he continued to battle hard."

On asked why his team scored much better in the second half than in the first (15 points in the first, 37 in the second), Miller replied, "Once we started the second half, we started getting the ball into Alan a lot easier, because they (South) extended their defense. They had to extend to pick up the tempo and that gave us the inside game."

"This was a tough loss after coming all this way," said a dejected and tired-looking Pat Rady. "They did a good job of taking us out of our offense. We got good shots, but they just wouldn't fall for us today."

Rady echoed Miller on South's extended defense. "Once we got down six to eight points we had to come out of the zone and play more aggressively on defense. They were going to be content to move it around the perimeter, and so we had to go out and get them.''

If ever there was a true David and Goliath story, a possible Cinderella fairy tale, the afternoon game was surely it. Gary Roosevelt, the largest of the four schools with an enrollment of 1,706, faced Whitko, enrollment 639. Whitko had no starter over 6-foot-4. The tallest player was 6-foot-5. Roosevelt, on the other hand, had Robinson at 6-foot-9 and Carlos Floyd at 6-foot-5. Most of the state had never heard of Whitko, but just about everybody had heard of Robinson, the Parade All-American. Roosevelt had suffered only one defeat, Whitko eight, the most of the four teams present. For Whitko, here was a chance to walk in the shoes of Milan; for Roosevelt the challenge was not to look past the Wildcats in search of Alan Henderson and Brebeuf.

Pull out your road atlas and look at the northeastern part of Indiana. See Ft. Wayne? Now, let your eye go due west along Highway 14 and you will run right into it. South Whitley. That is the home of the Whitko Wildcats.

Consolidated twenty years ago from Larwill, Pierceton, Sidney, and South Whitley high schools, Whitko sits near the border of Whitley and Kosciusko counties, hence Whit-Ko.

Except for perhaps the Whitko fans, no one really expected Whitko to emerge from the South Bend semistate. But favorites such as Concord and South Bend Riley fell by the wayside, and Whitko kept right on rolling.

The Wildcats steamrolled through the Columbia City sectional wasting Ft. Wayne Blackhawk by 26 and Manchester by 11. At the Ft. Wayne regionals Whitko squeaked by Ft. Wayne South Side by 3 and New Haven by 1. Up at South Bend, at the semistate played at the University of Notre Dame, the Wildcats crushed highly regarded LaPorte by 14 and beat big bad Marion, the winner of six state championships, by 9.

Their secret? A guard/forward named Steve Nicodemus. The 6-foot-4 senior averaged 29.3 ppg and 8.5 rpg. The Wildcats' starting center, 6-foot-2, 165-pound Chad Darley, averaged 11.1 ppg.

The Gary Roosevelt pep band pounded out a tune as the two teams walked out to midcourt. Whitko was designated as the visiting team. The players slapped hands and Robinson and Nicodemus stepped inside the circle. The tip went to Roosevelt.

Whitko opened with a 2-3 zone, keeping Robinson between Nicodemus and Darley. Both teams were nervous. Roosevelt's Jeffery Graham tossed up a hurried shot. Whitko rebounded, but Nicodemus walked. Robinson missed, then on Whitko's ensuing possession, Darryl Woods of Roosevelt stole the ball only to lose it. Finally, Whitko got on the board when Rich Tenney hit a jumper in the lane at the 6:34 mark.

Thirty seconds later Woods answered with a 15-foot jumper from the left side to tie the game. But then Roosevelt went cold and Whitko stormed out to an 8-0 run. During the spurt Roosevelt tossed up seven shots, all bricks. Whitko, meanwhile, hit everything they put up. Tenney drilled a 17-footer from the right side and Nicodemus laid one in for an easy two. Chad Ousley connected on a 10-foot jumper from the right side, and Nicodemus took a bounce pass from Darley, spun around, fired, and banked in a seven-footer. The score was 10–2 with 4:15 remaining and the dome was rocking.

Robinson finally broke the ice for the Panthers when Woods fed him a pass and he hit a turnaround jumper from the lane.

Chad Ousley then drove for a layup on a dish from Tenney to give the Wildcats a 12–4 lead with 3:30 remaining, but then Whitko dried up. Not until the 1:10 would they score again.

Roosevelt went to work. In the final 3:15 the Panthers romped for a 10-1 run. First, Robinson wowed the crowd with a monstrous jam. Next, Woods took a bounce-pass from Antonio Lee and nailed a 19-foot jumper, followed by Carlos Floyd banking home a 7-footer. Robinson then tied the game at 12 at the 2:00 mark with a turnaround jumper from the right side.

Lee fouled Rodney Thomas, sending Thomas to the line for a one-and-bonus. He hit the first, but the second lipped off. Whitko was back on top 13–12. But not for long.

Carlos Floyd shot a seven-footer, but it clanged high off the rim. Robinson jumped high to rebound, landed, and then went back up strong for the slam. Whitko inbounded, but Darley walked.

On the ensuing play Robinson flipped a pass to Lee who connected on a 19-foot jumper giving Roosevelt a 16–13 lead with twenty-two seconds remaining. The Panthers had bounced back from their 10–2 deficit, making it seem like long ago.

Roosevelt started the second quarter where they had left off at the end of the first. The Panthers jumped out to a 6–2 run on two baskets from Harding and another from Floyd giving Roosevelt a 22–15 lead with 4:20 remaining.

Whitko finally woke up when Nicodemus hit a short jumper in the lane to make it 22–17. Graham answered with a 16-foot jumper from the right side. Chad Ousley then laid one in on a dish from Tenney, and was fouled on the play by Harding. Ousley converted the free throw for the three-point play. On the ensuing possession Roosevelt turned it over when Lee tried to force it inside to Robinson. Darley stole it, flipped it to Nicodemus who laid it in. The Wildcats were back to within 24–22 with 2:24 left in the first half.

But that was all that Whitko would score in the quarter. Graham hit an 18-footer with 2:10 remaining and Robinson ended the half on an exclamation point when he stuffed one home off a missed jumper from the left side by Floyd. Intermission saw the No. 1 team in the state leading Whitko 28–22.

Whitko had to be pleased. They were setting the tempo of the game, had slowed Robinson to 10 first-half points (2 in the second quarter), and did not allow Roosevelt to the free-throw line at all in the first half. If the Wildcats could improve their free-throw shooting (2 for 7 in the first half) and cut down the turnovers (11), the game could still be theirs. And what happened last week at the South Bend semistate couldn't be overlooked, either. The Wildcats had been down 15 to Marion at half and had come back to beat them by 9.

But Roosevelt had had enough. Enough of this slow tempo, half-court stuff. They wanted to fly. And they did it with defense.

In the first five and a half minutes of the third quarter Roosevelt put on an awesome display of fastbreak basketball and scrappy defense that pressured the ball and shut down the passing lanes.

Jeffrey Graham was on fire from the outside, popping 2 three-pointers and hitting three more jumpers for a total of 12 third-quarter points. On the inside, Robinson put eight more points on the board, including a couple of spectacular jams. Harding, too, helped on the inside with 6 third-quarter points.

Whitko, on the other hand, was stifled. They couldn't get shots off, because of the pressure on the ball. When they did manage to get a shot off it was taken off balance or was not a shot like they had taken in the first half. Whitko could only manage 40-percent shooting, compared to Roosevelt's 74 percent. Nicodemus and Chad Ousley kept the Wildcats from embarrassment by scoring six points each. But the Wildcats were getting pounded on the boards (12–3). When Whitko coach Bill Patrick called his first time-out at the 4:34 mark, Whitko was still within a respectable distance, down only 39–31. But by his next time-out, at the 2:37 mark, he might as well have packed up and gone home. His team had managed only two points since his previous time-out, while the Velt had sprung for another 11. The score was 50–35, and by the end of the quarter the Panthers were up by 20, 58–38. It was midnight for Cinderella.

The fourth quarter was merely a formality. Fans began leaving halfway through the period with Roosevelt cruising on a 31-point lead. Robinson came out at the 4:13 mark after running a layup and sinking the subsequent foul shot. He finished with 23 points, 17 rebounds, 3 blocked shots, and 1 steal.

When the horn finally sounded the scoreboard read 83–53. It was the widest margin of victory in a Final Four game since Muncie Central routed Bloomington 102–66 back in 1960.

For Roosevelt, the good news about the win was the play of their guards. In the two games at the East Chicago regional and the two games at the Lafayette semistate Roosevelt's guards had combined for 46 of the 278 points scored, or a mere 16.5 percent. In the Whitko game the guards combined for 28 points. On the inside Roosevelt was unstoppable with Robinson; if Roosevelt's guards produced as they did in this game, beating Roosevelt would be very, very difficult.

"Our guards have been real consistent this year," said coach Heflin, seated next to IHSAA sports information director Bob Williams in the press room. "They have been consistently poor offensively. Today they played their usual good defense, but also produced offensively. I was glad to see that.

"Graham can stroke the ball," he continued. "The secret is to get the inside people to work. If they double off inside on Glenn and Carlos, he (Graham) will get his shots.

"I knew Whitko would try to slow it down. But we can play both ways. We can pressure and play a half-court game, too. We just don't come down the floor and put it up. We can slow it down, too. Now the guys *like* to play up-tempo, but if it's not then we'll adjust. The mark of a good team is the ability to adjust."

"No way we could get down 16 to a team of this caliber," said Whitko coach Bill Patrick, now in his twentieth year at Whitko. "We played well in the first half, but size was the difference in this game. Put 4 to 5 more inches on Nicodemus and he could play with Robinson. They were just too big. I haven't seen a better basketball team in quite awhile. He (Robinson) looked like an All-American today, that's for sure. He can shoot, dribble, feed the outlet pass, bring it down the floor, he can do it all.

"The third quarter was the key," Patrick continued. "What choice do you have? If you lay off Robinson he's gonna bury you, but if their guards are hitting like they were today you gotta go out after them, opening up the middle. We were counting on their guards not shooting well. No way we could stop the two inside players, so we tried to stop the guards, but they were on fire."

And so the last piece was in place for the matchup between Brebeuf and Roosevelt. It would be Alan against Glenn in the championship game at 8:05 pm.

The word out on the street was that Roosevelt would prevail. Conversation in the restaurants, bars, and hotels seemed to agree that Henderson was all Brebeuf had on the inside and maybe out front as well. Henderson would at least be able to hold his own against Robinson one-on-one, but Brebeuf would be unable to handle both Robinson *and* Floyd inside. And if Roosevelt's guards played Brebeuf the same way they played Whitko, then it was all over. The key was Roosevelt's guards.

The numbers seemed to bear this out. Robinson, Floyd, and Harding together averaged 51.5 ppg. Graham, Woods, and Wedlow together averaged 17.2. Brebeuf, on the other hand, had only one player averaging in double figures and that was Henderson at 28 ppg. No one else was even close. For Brebeuf to win, Henderson needed to get his points and at least slow down Robinson. Roosevelt's guards would have to revert to their usual lackadaisical self on offense, and Brebeuf would have to slow the tempo of the game in order to attempt only high-percentage shots.

A few minutes before eight o'clock a group of dancers from Floyd Central High School entertained the fans. The Dazzlers, as this group of girls was called, were dressed in green and gold tights and entertained the crowd of 30,345 for about five minutes. Then the Floyd Central boys a cappella choir, decked out in full choir robes, sang the national anthem.

With many fans on their feet, Robinson and Henderson approached the jump circle and slapped hands. Henderson tucked in his jersey, looked around, and stepped into the circle. Robinson was there waiting for him. The ball was tossed, and the tip went to the Braves.

Roosevelt fell into their usual man-to-man defense. Brebeuf's Greg Barber took the game's first shot, but it rimmed off to Roosevelt. The Panthers came down the floor, but Graham threw it away. Brebeuf was unable to score, sending Roosevelt back down the floor. But Henderson stole the ball, got it to forward Larry Winters who laid it in for two.

Robinson responded with a layup of his own on a feed from Graham with 6:42 showing. On the ensuing possession Henderson took a bad shot, missed, got his own rebound, but stepped out-of-bounds.

Winters hit again on a short jumper from a nice pass from David Roberts to make it 4–2. Robinson missed a turnaround jumper. Brebeuf rebounded, but Brad Hostetter walked. He redeemed himself, though, on the next play when he stole the ball from Graham and drove in for the layup to make it 6–2. On the ensuing possession Floyd was stuffed by Henderson. Brebeuf came up with zero on their next possession, and Robinson wowed the crowd with a big-time slam to make it 6–4.

Brebeuf's David Roberts tried to unload from inside, but Robinson cleanly swatted it away. Brebeuf got the ball back, but Henderson walked. Officials called time-out at 2:48.

Henderson was 0–3 to that point, while Robinson was 2–4. Brebeuf was playing the game everyone expected, a slower, deliberate game in search of the high-percentage shot.

When play resumed Hostetter picked off a Darryl Woods pass to Robinson. Hostetter threw it to Henderson who laid it in for his first two points to make the score 8–4.

Carlos Floyd answered when he rebounded a missed shot from Graham and put it back up and in at the 1:48 mark. Down the floor came Brebeuf. Henderson posted up, and the two battled each other for position, with Henderson yelling for the ball. Hostetter lobbed it into him, and Henderson turned, jumped, and shot, but Robinson blocked it cleanly. Henderson picked up the ball and immediately went up again, but Robinson blocked it again, and the crowd roared.

Roosevelt got the ball, but was unable to score. With two seconds remaining in the quarter, Robinson fouled Barber going up for a jumper in the lane. Barber hit the first free throw, but missed the second, and the quarter ended in Brebeuf's favor, 9–6.

The second quarter was an exercise in slow-down basketball by Brebeuf. But they might have slowed it down just a wee bit much. The Braves attempted only two field goals in the entire quarter, and they scored only one point. Roosevelt didn't help themselves, either. Poor shooting, 4 of 12, prevented them from capitalizing on Brebeuf's anemic offense.

Roosevelt inbounded to start the second quarter, and Brebeuf fell into the same man-to-man defense they used in the first quarter. Robinson tried shooting over Henderson, but it wouldn't fall. Forty seconds later he tried the same thing, and the result was still the same. Finally, Robinson stole the ball, pitched it to Harding, who bounced it to Graham who went in for the layup.

On the next possession Harding stole the ball from Hostetter. Harding got the ball to Robinson who was fouled by Roberts in the act of shooting. Robinson tied the game at nine with his first free throw, but he missed the second. The clock showed 6:06 remaining in the half.

Both teams now played "turnover." For the next three minutes neither team scored as bad passes, walks, and steals that were not converted took the limelight. Not that either team had their chances. At the 3:51 mark Henderson posted up Robinson, faked to his right, and drove left beating Robinson to the baseline and went in for a reverse layup. He missed, but Robinson fouled him, Robinson's only foul of the game. Henderson stepped to the line for two shots, but missed them both.

Robinson finally broke the ice when he hit a short jumper in the lane off a feed from Antonio Lee. That gave Roosevelt their first lead of the game at 11–9 with 3:33 left.

Floyd made back-to-back steals from Roberts and Winters, but was unable to convert, primarily because of good defense from Henderson, slapping away one of the shots. The officials then called timeout.

When play resumed Floyd nailed a 14-foot jumper just right of the key, and thirty seconds later Harding laid in a missed shot from Graham to extend the lead to 15–9. Henderson was not posting now, but playing away from the basket.

Brebeuf came up empty on their trip down the floor, then Robinson was called for offensive goaltending on a Carlos Floyd jumper.

With fifty-four seconds remaining in the half, Floyd fouled Hostetter who went to the line for one-and-one. He sank the first, the first Brebeuf point of the quarter, but missed the second. Roosevelt took the ball downcourt and ran down the clock. With the clock running down Robinson shot a turnaround jumper from about six feet, but missed. The half ended with Roosevelt up 15–10.

As in the Brebeuf–Terre Haute South game, the low scoring didn't sit well with many fans. "This is ridiculous," cried an unidentified fan, "they should bring in a shot clock."

The slowed-down game was what Brebeuf wanted, but they were still behind. Henderson was not getting his points (he had 2), and he was not getting any help from anyone else, either. Winters and Hostetter both had three points each, while Roberts had two. The good news was that Brebeuf was more than holding their own on the boards. The Braves had 17, with Henderson leading the way with 7. Roosevelt had 16 rebounds, Robinson with 6.

However, Brebeuf could not repeat the kind of game they played in the first half, or else they would surely lose. Roosevelt proved they could play the slow-tempo game and still be successful. Brebeuf, then, had to pick up the pace in order to put points on the board. But such a game definitely favored the Panthers for two reasons: (1) the Panthers enjoyed the faster game and played it well, and (2) Brebeuf, not accustomed to the faster game, was not in condition to keep up with Roosevelt. Nevertheless, Brebeuf coach Mike Miller, in his sixth year as head coach, had no choice. He had to speed it up. Henderson playing away from the basket late in the second quarter was an augur of this thinking.

The second half opened quickly with Robinson putting back in a missed shot from Floyd. Henderson answered with a 16-foot jumper from the baseline with 7:17 showing on the clock. But Brebeuf disappeared for the next three minutes, not scoring a point and committing six turnovers in the same amount of time. Roosevelt, meanwhile, rattled off 14 unanswered points starting with Harding nailing a short jumper from the baseline. Floyd hit one of his own from nearly the same spot, then stole the ball from Henderson who flipped it to Woods who passed it to Robinson who scored with a jumper from the free-throw line. Fastbreak basketball at its best, and Brebeuf called time-out to mull it over, down 23–12.

When play resumed Barber walked sending the ball back to Roosevelt. Floyd promptly scored with an 18-foot jumper just right of the key. On the ensuing possession Henderson bobbled the ball, Graham stole it, heaved it out to Robinson who laid it up for two, extending the lead to 27–12. Thirty seconds later Floyd connected on a short jumper from a feed from Robinson. On the ensuing possession Henderson again lost the handle. Graham came up with it, and passed it to Harding. Henderson, meanwhile, had raced down the floor and was able to block the jumper Harding attempted.

With 4:22 showing on the clock Robinson was fouled by Roberts. As he stepped to the free-throw line, the normally unemotional Robinson waved the crowd to pick up the noise. Then he calmly sank both ends of the two-shot foul giving Roosevelt a 19-point lead, 31–12. But Roosevelt would not score again in the quarter.

Brebeuf finally broke their dry spell when Henderson scored on a reverse layup, moving deftly around Robinson. Barber then nailed a 17-foot jumper from the left side to make it 31–16.

Roosevelt's next trip down the floor was fruitless, but Henderson threw it away on the ensuing possession, giving the ball back to Roosevelt. But Robinson fumbled the ball, and Barber stole it and passed it to Courtney who got it to Henderson who laid it up and in. Twenty-six seconds later Winters laid another in on a feed from Hostetter to make it 31–20 with 1:42 remaining in the period.

With three seconds showing on the clock Roosevelt's Rickie Wedlow went hard to the basket, but Henderson blocked it big time. Robinson picked up the ball and went up hard himself, but Henderson tied him up, and the ref called jump ball. Possession Brebeuf. Barber received the inbounds pass, but he was called for palming the ball. The quarter ended with Roosevelt on top 31–20.

Roosevelt wasted no time putting points on the board at the start of the fourth quarter. Seven seconds after the inbounds pass Floyd sank a 13-foot jumper. Brebeuf's Brian Anderson then forced a poor pass into the middle, and Robinson picked it off. Robinson flipped it to Harding who was fouled by Barber, and Harding went to the free-throw line to shoot two. He hit both, making the score 35–20 with only twenty-eight seconds having been played in the period.

Brebeuf finally got on the board when Henderson broke loose, dribbled behind his back to fake out Robinson and laid it in for two, being fouled on the play by Robinson. But Henderson missed the subsequent free throw.

On the ensuing possession Robinson posted up Henderson, and Robinson executed one of his turnaround jumpers, but Henderson committed his first foul by hacking him on the play, forcing the ball to veer way off. Robinson stepped to the line for two, missing the first, but making the second. Roosevelt by 14, 36–22, with 7:06 remaining.

On the next possession Larry Courtney laid one in for Brebeuf, but Roosevelt then rattled off eight straight points that, in effect, broke Brebeuf's spirit. First, Antonio Lee connected on a 12-footer in the lane. Then Lee followed that with a layup. Next, Robinson grabbed a long rebound and heaved it to Floyd who laid it in for two. Now Roosevelt was pumped, they began to smell it, and the players as well as the Roosevelt fans began slapping high-fives, pumping their fists, and clapping their hands. Floyd was fouled on the play by Barber, but he missed the subsequent free throw. Eighteen seconds later Robinson stole the ball from Anderson. Robinson flipped it to Harding who fired it up, but missed. Robinson rebounded, slamming it home, and Roosevelt had stretched their lead to 20 points, 44–24, with 5:30 left.

Brebeuf—looking tired and Henderson appearing frustrated—finally scored on a short jumper by Winters. But Courtney fouled Harding on the next play. Harding sank both ends of the one-and-one pushing Roosevelt's lead back up to 20, 46–26.

At the 4:42 mark Henderson stole the ball from Lee. Henderson passed it to Barber who bounced it back to Henderson who went over Robinson for the layup. Roosevelt called time-out; their fans roaring their approval.

When play resumed Hostetter stole the ball from Harding, but after Brebeuf brought the ball down the floor Lee stole the ball from Henderson. Down the other way they came where Henderson committed his second foul by slapping Robinson on the wrist. Robinson stepped to the line grinning. He took the ball from the ref and quickly buried both ends of the one-and-bonus. Roosevelt 48, Brebeuf 28.

Brebeuf's final field goal came with 2:55 remaining when Henderson shot a short jumper over Robinson's head. Now Roosevelt spread the floor and began playing keep away. With 2:34 showing, Harding appeared to have an open shot on the left side, but Henderson quickly moved over to him and blocked his shot.

Brebeuf's last points came at the 2:28 mark on a pair of free throws by Courtney who was fouled by Lee. Again the Panthers spread the floor and played keep away, sending the Roosevelt fans to their feet.

With 1:11 remaining, Courtney fouled Woods who went to the line for a one-and-one. He hit the front end, but missed the second, making the score 49–32. The Roosevelt fans began singing, ''Hey hey good-bye.''

At the 45-second mark Roberts fouled Robinson. Heflin pulled his players and sent in the bench. Floyd, Harding, Woods, and Lee came off the floor to hug Heflin, then waved frantically at the roaring of the fans.

Robinson, meanwhile, stepped to the free-throw line, his face once more set in a grin. He sank both ends of the one-and-one making it 51–32. Appropriately, it was Robinson who scored the last points of the 1990–91 Indiana high school basketball season.

After the free throws the horn blared again, and Robinson lifted his arms in the air, acknowledging the crowd's cheers. He hugged Heflin, slapped hands and hugged his teammates, then sat down. His high school career was now complete.

A crowd of players, coaches, cheerleaders, and photographers milled around the makeshift stage hastily erected on the court. The Roosevelt fans were cheering, ''We're number one!''

Brebeuf received their runners up medals and trophy first. Each player walked across the stage to accept the award.

Roosevelt was next. They lined up single file, players first then coaches, and walked across the stage. The cheerleaders laughed and smiled and cried and hugged down on the floor below. When the team trophy was handed out Robinson and Floyd held it high to show the fans, stretching it even higher over their heads to show the fans way up in the upper decks of the huge dome.

Standing on the court watching all of this was an older man wearing a dark suit. He wore glasses, and his hair was flecked with gray. As each member of the Roosevelt team walked across the stage and as Robinson and Floyd held high the team trophy, this man smiled. Once again he was part of a championship team, although this time admittedly in an indirect way. Nevertheless, he was there on the floor surrounded by the Indiana high school state champs, just as he was back in '68.

That was why Louis ''Bo'' Mallard was smiling.

Someone else was standing on the floor, too. Someone who was finally a part of a championship team. He was not officially an assistant basketball coach at Gary Roosevelt, but he came to every practice to help coach Heflin with the team, and he sat with the team at games as well. He was filling the same role that Heflin had filled under Mallard back in 1968.

The championship ring had been within his grasp not once, but twice; not just in high school, but at a major college as well. But he had fallen short, this person, missing the glory by only that much.

Now, standing among Robinson and Floyd and Harding and Heflin and the others, he was redeemed. He had his championship.

Flash back to 1982. The championship game of the state finals at Market Square Arena in Indianapolis. His team, Gary Roosevelt, had a 62–60 lead over Plymouth with four seconds left in the game. Plymouth had possession of the ball. All Roosevelt had to do was make sure no one got off a good shot. Roosevelt made sure, but Plymouth's Scott Skiles launched a desperation 20-footer anyway. Swish, overtime.

At the end of the first overtime the game was still tied, so they went into double overtime. And though he scored the last bucket of the game and led Roosevelt with 19 points, it was not enough. Plymouth won the state championship by just one point, 75–74.

The following year he played for the University of Houston. Houston steamrolled through the regular season, through most of the NCAA tournament, and on Monday April 4 he again found himself on a team contending for a championship, this time for the national title against North Carolina State. Akeem Olajuwon, Larry Micheaux, Michael Young, and Clyde Drexler were on that Houston team, the so-called Phi Slama Jama.

At halftime of the championship game Houston trailed North Carolina State 33–25. But Houston fought its way back, and with less than five seconds left in the game Houston and N.C. State were tied at 52.

Then it happened. North Carolina State's Derick Whittenburg launched a last-gasp shot from midcourt. Seeing that it would fall short, Lorenzo Charles leaped high, caught the ball in the air, and slammed it home for the national title. N.C. State 54, Houston 52.

The freshman from Gary Roosevelt High School couldn't believe it. Once again, just a year later in fact, a championship seemingly within his grasp had slipped from his fingers. He fell to the floor, and what is etched in the memory of every college basketball fan's mind thanks to television is the picture of him falling to his knees, his left hand covering his tear-streaked face, his right hand slapping the floor over and over again in frustration, bitterness, and sorrow. Lightning had struck twice.

But now it was 1991, and he was standing on the floor of the Hoosier Dome, and he was surrounded by deliriously happy people, and he was happy, too. No sudden losses to swallow, no what-might-have-beens to rehash when he was all alone.

Renaldo Thomas got his championship at last.

"The most important factor in the game was fatigue," said coach Heflin, again sitting on the raised table in the press room. "I knew if we kept pressing and running, pressing and running we would eventually wear them down, and that is what happened. We wanted to keep up the up-tempo game, and the referees let them play the physical game that we like.

"They wanted to slow down our up-tempo style and they kept it close in the first half," Heflin continued. "I knew they would wear down in the second half. They did not have the conditioning to play with us the entire game.

"The third time was the charm, I guess. I kept more seniors on this team than I normally would have because I knew we had a chance to get here this season."

Robinson walked into the press room arm-in-arm with his mother. She stood off to the side as her son mounted the steps to the table.

"I was not out to make an impression on anybody today," Robinson said into the microphone. "I just wanted to win the state title. I did not think about the matchup with Alan, I was just focusing on winning the game.

"I did whatever I had to do to get Alan out of his game," Robinson continued. "I knew if I could keep him to around 14 to 15 points, we had a chance to win the game and that is how it turned out. I did not care about winning Mr. Basketball. I would have traded Mr. Basketball to win the state championship."

After Robinson and Heflin departed, Brebeuf coach Mike Miller and Alan Henderson stepped forward.

"Their defensive pressure was the difference," Miller said. "We never got into the flow of the game offensively. They did to us what we normally do to teams. For awhile I thought it would be an incredible defensive struggle. It was 9 to 9 for a long time. We turned it over a few times, and it got to be too big a mountain to climb."

Then Henderson spoke. "I was really excited about the game, playing against Glenn and Gary Roosevelt," said Henderson. "They were a better team than us offensively and defensively. I learned that things don't always go your way. I'll bounce back. Maybe next year we'll win the championship. We're all winners. Each one of us will go on and be successful. Glenn has a lot of athletic ability, a turnaround jump shot, and is strong inside.

"Hopefully, I'll get Mr. Basketball," Henderson continued. "But if I don't it'll give me more incentive to work harder."

The numbers for Robinson and Henderson: 22 points, 10 rebounds, 3 blocked shots, and 4 steals for Robinson; 14 points, 10 rebounds, 5 blocked shots, and 3 steals for Henderson.

The only other player in double figures for Roosevelt besides Robinson was, of course, Carlos Floyd with 12. No one but Henderson scored in double figures for Brebeuf.

Roosevelt outrebounded Brebeuf 27–25, and Roosevelt forced Brebeuf into 28 turnovers. The Panthers committed 15.

The combined 83 points of the game tied the lowest total points scored in a championship game since 1953 when South Bend Central defeated Terre Haute Gerstmeyer 42–41. The 32 points scored by Brebeuf equaled the lowest point total by a school since 1954 when Milan defeated Muncie Central 32–30.

One last thing remained before the party was over, and that was to award the Arthur L. Trester Mental Attitude Award. The Trester Award medal is given each year to an outstanding senior basketball player for leadership, scholarship, athletic ability, and mental attitude.

The medal has been awarded each year since 1945. Prior to that year, the award was known as the Gimbel Medal for Mental Attitude. The Gimbel award stretched back to 1917.

With Brebeuf in the championship game, and with Henderson being such an outstanding student, most believed he was a lock for the Trester Award. But if not Henderson, at least *someone* from Brebeuf. The school was, after all, a Jesuit-run college prep institution known for its academics.

So when Steve Nicodemus, the star from Whitko, was announced as the recipient, the Whitko fans, those left anyway, roared with delight.

Nicodemus, from South Whitley, was the state's third-leading scorer with a 29.3 average. He was also an all-conference (Three Rivers) football player and an all-conference baseball player. He was active in student council and the South Whitley Methodist Church.

15

Mr. Basketball

He was in Springfield, Massachusetts when he learned that he had been named Mr. Basketball of Indiana. He was in Springfield playing in the fourteenth annual McDonald's High School All-Star game, scoring 20 points, helping the West team defeat the East 108–106. His competition for the title of Mr. Basketball, the player who had dogged him the entire season, was also in Springfield, playing in the same game on the same team. That was on a Saturday.

On the following Monday afternoon, April 8, the *Indianapolis Star* made it official. In a press conference in the Community Room of Roosevelt High School Pat Aikman of the *Indianapolis Star,* game director of the Indiana-Kentucky All-Star series, introduced Glenn Robinson as Indiana's 1991 Mr. Basketball. The presentation marked the first time the *Star* had gone to the recipient high school to present the award. The remainder of the All-Star team would be named three weeks later.

A handful of press, friends, and school administrators applauded as Robinson, clad in his No. 1 All-Star jersey, stepped up to the podium to say a few words. The 6-foot-9 Purdue-bound Mr. Basketball had to bend down to speak into the microphone that seemed to reach to his navel.

"This is a great honor, and I'm glad to have it," Robinson said. "I thank the voters and especially coach Heflin. In every category during the year Alan (Henderson) was beating me. Coach said we have to go far in the state tournament in order to prove myself. He told me, 'don't change your game. Play the way you have been playing and everything will be all right.' And it was.

"But I feel better about winning the state championship," Robinson continued, "I was focused on that first and next Mr. Basketball."

Robinson became the second person from Roosevelt High School to be named Mr. Basketball. William "Jake" Eison was awarded the title back in 1955. Eison scored 31 points in a 97–74 loss to an Oscar Robertson-led Crispus Attucks team in the 1955 state championship game. Robertson scored 30 points in that game. Robertson won Mr. Basketball the following year.

Eison was present at the Monday afternoon press conference for Robinson.

"It took thirty-six years for Gary to get another Mr. Basketball," said Eison, "but they got a good one. It was not such a big deal back when I got it."

Eison, who also played at Purdue, was asked to compare Glenn Robinson with Robertson.

"He's up there with him," Eison said, raising his eyebrows. "Oscar was big, but played guard. Glenn can handle the ball, too, for a kid his size. He's an all-around player. He can do the boards, bring it down the floor, he seems to be a team player as Oscar was."

Eison also remarked on the changes in the game since he played at Roosevelt.

"Well, the game is faster, now," Eison said. "The big guys can handle the ball better now. When I played, the big men just posted up and that was it. Now they're more like Glenn, handling the ball, going outside, bringing it down the floor."

Robinson said his plans for the summer were to play against the Soviets on a Lafayette AAU team and to play on an AAU team in Florida.

Robinson also had plans to take a test. The Saturday following the press conference Robinson was scheduled to take his Scholastic Aptitude Test for the third time.

When the press conference ended someone stood up who had been sitting in the front row, someone who had been seated next to Robinson, in fact. During the press conference he had remained silent, for no one had asked him anything. He milled around a little bit afterwards, chatting with those present, then walked out of the room.

Coach Heflin nodded his head towards Carlos Floyd, and as Carlos left the room Heflin said, "We couldn't have done it without Carlos, no way. He was the team leader. He was the one that talked to the kids on the court, gathered them in the huddles. Glenn led by example, but Carlos led by talking to the team, encouraging them, getting on their butts when they slacked off. He'll do well at Idaho State."

Heflin placed his hands on his hips and looking down at the floor said, "I'm gonna miss him."

The vote wasn't even close. Robinson received 198¹/₂ votes, while Alan Henderson picked up 130¹/₂. Of the 647 ballots mailed to the state's high school coaches and media, 329 were returned. A little more than half.

Going into the state championship game Henderson was thought by many to hold the edge on winning Mr. Basketball. But that changed after the title game. Robinson was clearly the dominating force between the two. Pat Aikman said that 40 percent of the ballots were returned after the state finals, indicating that many wanted to see a possible matchup between the two contenders. Although Aikman would not divulge the voting that came in prior to the state finals, he did say that those ballots coming in after the game heavily favored Robinson.

Some believed that a Co-Mr. Basketball should have been named, for the difference between the two, they said, was just too thin. For the two-game state finals Robinson scored 45 points (18 of 34, 52.9%), grabbed 27 rebounds, and blocked 5 shots. Henderson scored 40 points (15 of 32, 46.8%), grabbed 33 rebounds, and blocked 6 shots. Both were the top players in the state, no one else even coming close. Bill Benner, a columnist for the Indianapolis *Star,* argued in the March 24 Sunday *Star* (the day following the state finals) for the Co-Mr. Basketball, saying the difference between the two players was minimal, that both were deserving.

But Aikman stated early on that a Co-Mr. Basketball would be named only in the event of a tie vote. That, of course, did not happen. Benner wrote another column in the Sunday April 7 issue of the *Star,* the day Mr. Basketball was announced in the newspapers, stating that a Co–Mr. Basketball award would have been preferable. He said that he had split his vote between Robinson and Henderson.

"...I could not see how the argument could be made that one was better than the other and, therefore, more deserving of one of the most coveted awards in this state," Benner wrote.

For years the *Star* wouldn't announce the vote totals for Mr. Basketball, as if the votes were some sort of holy ballot. Only the Vatican, when electing a new pope, insisted on greater secrecy. On those rare occasions when the votes for Mr. Basketball were extremely tight the *Star* simply called the vote a tie and declared a Co–Mr. Basketball. Whether there actually was a tie nobody knows.

Since the inception of the award back in 1939, a Co–Mr. Basketball has been presented four times. The first time was in 1961 when the twins Dick and Tom Van Arsdale of Indianapolis Manual were both given the award. In 1974 Roy Taylor of Anderson and Steve Collier of Southwestern (Hanover) were named Co–Mr. Basketball. Delray Brooks of Michigan City Rogers and Troy Lewis of Anderson were named in 1984, and Jay Edwards and Lyndon Jones, both from Marion, snapped it up in 1987.

OFF-SEASON

16

All-Star Games

Summer in the Ohio River Valley always brings out the three Hs: hazy, hot, and humid weather. More often than not the summer haze sits around all fat and sassy, gleefully making life miserable, like an idiot neighbor who insists on sawing a trombone in half in the dead of night.

Summer brings out the big B, too. B as in basketball.

Some streets were blocked off to traffic just north of Broadway this past June in Louisville. And instead of cars crawling by, basketballs were being slammed and drilled into more than a score of portable basketball goals set up along the streets.

The Winn-Dixie Street Ball Showdown was two days of three-on-three matchups by nearly 4,000 Michael Jordan wannabes. The Showdown was divided into sixty-nine divisions and spanned two days. Visions of All-Stardom, no doubt, danced through their heads.

Meanwhile, a couple of miles south, inside Freedom Hall at the Kentucky Fair & Exposition Center, some real all-stars were going through their pregame warmups. And no doubt some visions were going through their heads as well. For these all-stars were the cream of the past season's senior class from the states of Indiana and Kentucky. Most would play ball in college next year, some at big-time programs like Indiana, Purdue, Vanderbilt, and Kentucky. Chances are these all-stars envisioned themselves on their college's home court, a court like the one they were on now, the home floor of the Cardinals of the University of Louisville. And maybe, just maybe, some of these all-stars were looking even beyond their college years, gazing instead toward the promised land, toward the floor of an NBA team like the one they had played upon just the week before at Market Square Arena in Indianapolis, the home of the Indiana Pacers. Heady stuff for an eighteen-year-old kid.

The Indiana-Kentucky High School All-Star Game is an annual summer affair. Indeed, this game marked the fiftieth time the two states had pitted teams against one another. Begun in 1940, the game has been presented annually except in the war years of 1943 and 1944.

"The World Series of High School Basketball," as the event likes to call itself, is a two-game affair: one game is played in Indianapolis, the other in Louisville or Lexington. The two-game format was started in 1955. Until then only one game was played each summer and that was in Indianapolis. Ironically, the first year two games were played Indiana won at Louisville and Kentucky won at Indianapolis. Indiana holds a substantial lead in the series, 55–32. The Indiana game is sponsored by the *Indianapolis Star,* while the Kentucky game is sponsored by the Lions Club. All proceeds are for the benefit of the blind. Two twenty-minute halves, as in college ball, are played rather than four quarters.

The All-Star game alumni is a veritable Who's Who of Basketball Land. The likes of Oscar Robertson, Larry Bird, Rick Mount, George McGinnis, Kent Benson, Steve Alford, Wes Unseld, Louis Dampier, Rex Chapman, and Shawn Kemp have put on quite a show these past fifty years. This year promises no less.

While the 1991 edition of the Kentucky All-Stars warm up with some routine layups, out trots the Indiana contingent to the cheers and applause of half of the 8,562 on hand. Since Louisville sits just across the Ohio River from Indiana, the turn out of Hoosier fans is always large. For the Indianapolis games the overall attendance is always larger, but the percentage of Kentucky fans is always less. The 12,595 that attended the previous week's game in Indianapolis, for example, was almost entirely Indiana fans. Indianapolis is at least two hours from Louisville, three hours from Lexington, and even longer from Owensboro, Paducah, Ashland, or Hazard, making the Indiana leg of the series primarily a Hoosier affair.

As the Indiana All-Stars trot around the court to begin their warmups, only one thing is on their minds, revenge. Kentucky stuck it to the Hoosiers in the first game 103–101, and the Indiana boys are feeling a bit miffed. They were supposed to have won in Indianapolis. They were bigger and stronger than Kentucky, and Glenn Robinson was easily the most talented player on either team.

Indiana had five players 6-foot-7 or taller: Glenn Robinson (Roosevelt, 6-9), Brian Evans (Terre Haute South, 6-8), Andy Elkins (Evansville Bosse, 6-7), Brandon Brantly (Andrean, 6-8), and Damon Beathea (Elkhart Memorial 6-7). One player conspicuously absent from the roster was Alan Henderson (6-8) who elected not to play in the All-Star game due to a prior commitment.

With all this muscle Indiana was supposed to dominate. But Kentucky coach Randy Embry had an idea. He'd run those Hoosier musclemen down to a frazzle.

"To get up and down the floor as quickly as possible," said Embry, "with our athletes that's the way we had to play."

And so they did.

Led by a pair of speedsters from Fairdale High School (the reigning Kentucky state champions), Maurice Morris (27 points) and Mr. Basketball Jermaine Brown (21 points, 13 rebounds), Kentucky bolted from the gate quickly and kept Indiana flat on its heels all night.

Indiana provided the rope for its own hanging by committing 19 turnovers, 12 in the first half, and shooting a paltry 16 of 31 (51.6 percent) from the free throw line. Indiana had difficulty getting back on defense, too. Not a few Kentucky points were scored by simple layups on three-on-two or two-on-one fast breaks. And for all the talk of Indiana's height, the Hoosiers grabbed only one more rebound than did the Bluegrass boys, 46–45.

"We knew they'd be quicker," said Jim Hahn of Concord, the Indiana coach, "but to make turnovers the way we did and shoot free throws the way we did, we shouldn't even have been in it."

Indiana was down only 50–47 at half. Marlon Fleming tied the game at 69 with 12:24 left in the second half by making one of two free throws, and a minute sixteen seconds later Indiana took its first lead of the game, 71–69, when Glenn Robinson took a pass from Ryan Wolf and slammed it home. Indiana stretched its lead to five, 75–70, with 9:39 left to play when Fleming tipped in a Steve Nicodemus misfire.

But the Kentuckians refused to fold. With only nineteen seconds left, and Indiana trailing Kentucky 99–95, Lamar Morton of Muncie South buried a three-pointer from the left corner to cut Kentucky's lead to one, 99–98. But Kentucky's Darrin Horn calmly sank two free throws to keep the Hoosiers at bay, and Indiana was unable to make up the difference. The Hoosiers lost on their home court.

Indiana's Mr. Basketball, Mr. Robinson, led Indiana with 26 points, 10 rebounds, but hit only 10 of 18 free throws before fouling out with thirty-two seconds left.

Jeff Massey of Concord was a bright spot for Indiana. He finished with 18 points, 6 assists, and 5 rebounds. He came off the bench to score 12 first-half points and finished the game with a team-high 28 minutes played. Marlon Fleming of Southport added 16 points to go along with his 5 boards.

About the only really good thing to be said about the Indiana effort at Market Square Arena was that Hoosiers Cole Casbon of Boone Grove High School won the Dunkin' Donuts Slam-Dunk Contest, and Tony Frieden from Manchester High School captured the Domino's Pizza Showcase Shootout 3-point contest. Of course, no Kentuckians competed in either one of those events.

It was time to regroup.

But that didn't come too easily. Robinson and guard LaSalle Thompson didn't show up for practice the Tuesday morning following the Indianapolis game. "We didn't know where they were," said Hahn. So Hahn benched the two for Wednesday night's exhibition game in Martinvsville against something called the Hoosier All-Stars, a team made up of ex-college players Steve Alford, Jerry Sichting, Dan Palombizio, and others. The old-timers kicked the Indiana All-Stars' butt off the floor, 130–88. When practice did resume the players and coaches were "walking around on egg shells," as one reporter put it who was present at the practices, trying not to bruise the egos being worn on shirt sleeves, or in this case basketball jerseys. Fun was definitely not the word to describe the Indiana camp. Perhaps boot camp was better.

But it was a boot camp filled with a sense of purpose, to regain some pride.

"We talked about having a lot of pride," said Hahn. "This game is important to Indiana and Kentucky. You have to give the kids credit for keeping faith and keeping their intensity."

But moments after the opening tip of the Louisville game, Indiana seemed anything but intense. Just as in the opening of the Indianapolis game, Kentucky jumped out to a quick lead in this game. Before ninety seconds had ticked away the Bluegrass boys owned a 7–2 lead.

Kentucky's speed seemed to fluster Indiana, and just as in the Indianapolis game the Hoosiers seemed to have trouble getting back on defense.

But Indiana settled down, and Kentucky went dry. After Kentucky went up 17–12 with 14:42 remaining in the first half, Indiana went on a 14–4 run in a span of four minutes. Indiana took its first lead, 21–19, at the 10:43 mark, when LaSalle Thompson nailed a three-pointer from the right corner. The Hoosiers went on to score five unanswered points before Kentucky's Chris Harrison sank a jumper in the lane to make the score 26–21 in favor of Indiana.

Then the three-point bombs starting falling. Maurice Morris drilled a trey from the left side. Hoosier Ryan Wolf connected on a two-pointer from the left corner to maintain the Indiana lead 28–24. But Kentucky's Mr. Basketball, Jermaine Brown, nailed a three-pointer from the top of the key to bring Kentucky within 28–27 at the 7:50 mark. Twenty seconds later Chris Harrison dropped a three-pointer of his own and Kentucky was up 30–28.

In the next four minutes the score was tied three times. Indiana took its final lead of the half at the 2:47 mark when Glen Robinson hit the front end of a two shot foul to make the score 40–39.

With forty-five seconds remaining in the first period Kentucky grabbed a 47–42 lead on back-to-back jumpers by Dion Lee. However, Indiana headed to the locker room down only 47–45 when LaSalle Thompson hit a free throw, and Andy Elkins rebounded Thompson's second free throw attempt and put it in with only four seconds left in the half.

At half Indiana had three players in double figures. Jeff Massey had 13 points while Elkins and Robinson each had 10 points. Robinson also had 6 rebounds.

Kentucky, meanwhile, had only one player in double figures. Jermaine Brown had 13 points to go along with 5 rebounds.

Despite Indiana's height advantage, the Hoosiers were still getting out rebounded 24–15. Kentucky was shooting better, too, clipping along at 54 percent from the field, while Indiana was making only 51 percent of its shots from the floor. Both teams tossed up eight three-pointers. Kentucky connected on four, Indiana on two. Indiana was staying in the game at the free throw line. Kentucky only shot 5 free throws in the first half, making 3. Indiana, on the other hand, stepped to the free throw line 17 times, hitting 9.

Whatever Hahn and his assistant coaches Jack Butcher (Loogootee) and Jimmie Howell (Fortville) said to their team at half, it should be bottled and sold. Indiana came out much more aggressively in the second half and clearly dominated the game.

Indiana displayed its aggressiveness at the very beginning of the second half when Jeff Massey snagged an alley-oop pass from LaSalle Thompson and jammed it home only forty-five seconds into the half to tie the game at 47.

Kentucky's Bryan Milburn answered with a jumper, but Indiana scored the next four points to take a 51–49 lead. Kentucky then went on a 5–2 run to take a 54–53 lead at the 17:19 mark. But that was to be their last lead of the game.

Indiana went on a 11–0 run that put Indiana up 64–54 at the 14:15 mark. Kentucky would come no closer than four points the rest of the game. The whole second half was a series of runs for Indiana. They also put together 7–2 and 6–0 runs. The final was 98–86, Indiana.

The difference? Indiana's more aggressive play in the second half and Kentucky's poor shooting as a result of the Hoosier's intensity. Indiana was placing more pressure on the ball, contesting more loose balls, and fighting a little harder on the boards. As a result Kentucky shot only 36 percent from the field in the second half. However, not helping them was lack of visits to the free throw line. Kentucky only shot 8 free throws in the second half, making 6. Indiana, though, stepped to the line 16 times and hit 14.

Indiana also got more help on the boards in the second half. In the first half Robinson was doing all the work. In the second half Indiana's Mr. Basketball got some help from Andy Elkins (9) and Marlon "the Marlin" Fleming (5), the 6-foot-4 240-pound hulk bound for Ball State. However, Kentucky *still* managed to out rebound Indiana 47–41.

"We used Glenn as a decoy," said coach Hahn, "bringing him up a little higher and cutting Jeff [Massey] through the back door. Glenn contested a lot more shots in the second half, making them change their shots in mid stroke. I think that accounted for much of Kentucky's poor shooting in the second [half]."

Four Hoosiers scored in double figures. Leading all scorers was Robinson (26). Then came Massey (25), Elkins (15), and LaSalle Thompson (11).

Fittingly, it was Robinson who scored the final points in the 1990–91 high school basketball season. He stuffed a Jeff Massey misfire with 4.7 seconds remaining to bring his two-game All-Star combined score to 52.

Unfortunately, Robinson's score in a more important contest wasn't as impressive. One week after the All-Star game Robinson learned he had failed to meet the NCAA-mandated score of at least 18 on the American College Test (ACT) he had taken on June 8. That marked the third time he had failed the ACT. He had likewise failed to score the NCAA-mandated score of 700 on the Scholastic Aptitude Test (SAT) on two other occasions. Consequently, the 6-foot-9 Mr. Basketball was academically ineligible for the 1991–92 season at Purdue, the school he had signed with back in November 1990.

An augury of Robinson's plight came in the press room following the All-Star game in Louisville. A reporter asked Robinson if he would turn pro if he were ineligible for his freshman year at Purdue. Said Robinson without expression, "If I don't make my test scores, I'm still going to Purdue."

The headline on the front of the sports page of the *Gary Post-Tribune* on Sunday, June 30, asked, "Is Ineligibility a Blessing in Disguise?"

Ask Robinson two years from now at the start of the 1992–93 season.

17

Summer Camps

Forty-four second and third graders sat on the gym floor. Some sat cross-legged. Some sat with their feet flat on the floor, their arms clasped around their upright knees. Others leaned back on outstretched arms.

They all paid close attention to the man. All eyes focused on the man standing before them; the man with the beard and the basketball tucked under his arm; the man who was the head coach at Valparaiso High School. No one whispered to a buddy or stared blankly into space. This, after all, was not arithmetic or spelling.

These eight- and nine-year-old boys were clad in T-shirts bearing the likeness of Michael Jordan or the snorting bull of the NBA champion Chicago Bulls. They were shod in high-top Nikes or Converse.

Bob Punter, the man with the beard and the basketball tucked under his arm, looked down at the faces peering up at him. How often had he seen that gleam in the eye of a child? For a week, now, he had instructed these children in the rudiments of the game of basketball, how to pass, how to dribble, how to shoot. For an hour and fifteen minutes each day he showed them where to place their feet when shooting a free throw, how to cradle the ball for a jump shot, how to position for the rebound. He tried to instill in them the importance of teamwork. He stressed diligence and practice. He emphasized hard work.

Now the week was over, and he was groping for some words, some *thing* that would stay in the mind of an eight-year-old longer than the normal thirty to sixty seconds.

"Between now and next June," he said to them trying to look into the eye of each and every boy, "you have a chance to shoot 10,000 shots."

He paused. Then he continued, "Somebody will shoot those 10,000 shots. Somebody like a Larry Bird or a Steve Alford or a Michael Jordan."

Again he paused, allowing time for the mythical names to register. "Now, you can go home and sit down in front of the TV. You can go to the movies or you can play your computer games or go fishing. Or you can go outside and pick up your basketball."

Punter then turned around and pointed to some names up on the wall, names of Valparaiso High School Basketball players who had earned the honor of playing on the Indiana All-Star team. Forty-four pairs of eyes followed the swoop of his hand.

"In the year 2001 or so," he said, "your name could be up there."

And with that the camp was over.

Green T-shirts with "Valpo Basketball" printed in white letters were given to each boy as was a small certificate signed by Punter. Two trophies were handed out honoring he who made the most free throws and he who exhibited the best sportsmanship.

This is where it begins. The forging of the Glenn Robinsons, the Alan Hendersons, the Andy Elkins, the Sam Obermeyers begins here. Not just in Indiana, but nationwide kids attend similar camps. Camps for kids of all ages, from the second graders up through high school. Punter, for example, holds his camp in Valparaiso for second graders up through eighth graders.

Coaches watch the kids to see who's got it and who doesn't. The kids know the coach watches, they're not dumb, and the kids often wait until they know the coach is watching before drilling that three-pointer, leaping for that tough rebound, or faking out that defender. It's called showing your stuff. Now and then the coach will jot down a name on a legal pad, on a clipboard, or take some kid aside and ask him his name, what school he attends, and where he lives. Sometimes other coaches will come and watch. Bill Berger, for example, the head coach at LaCrosse High School was spotted sitting in on Punter's camp for seventh and eighth graders one afternoon. Coaches need to see who's out there and how good they really are. Their jobs as coaches depend on it.

The younger kids, the second and third graders, are really just learning the game, more often than not these camps are their first experience in organized ball. And it shows. Balls are dribbled of feet, double dribble is epidemic, passes resemble a pitcher's toss in slow pitch softball, shots either drop feet from the basket or ricochet off the bottom of the rim and smack the shooter back in the face. Games are little more than controlled chaos. Scores of 24–0, 32–2, 4–2, are common.

Patience is the key word when dealing with the little ones. One afternoon Punter watched his second and third graders practice shooting free throws. Simply wretched. So he decided they would learn more by not allowing them to use a ball. He lined them up on the baselines and sidelines, and using that as an imaginary free throw line he showed them where to place their feet, how far apart their feet should be (''I should be able to roll a basketball between your feet!''), how much bend there should be in the knees, the position of the wrist, etc. So for several minutes forty-four boys stood side by side around the Valparaiso gym practicing free throws without using a basketball.

''Follow through!'' Punter barked. ''Bend the knees. You should see a wrinkle in your wrist as you cradle the ball.'' Now and then he would stop and position a kid's feet or show him where his elbow should be or explain how he should keep his eye on the rim. It was school. It is doubtful, though, any of those kids thought of it as such.

One hundred and thirty miles south, in Indianapolis, another school was in session. One of the teachers in this school, a Mr. DiMassa from the David Starr Jordan High School of Long Beach, California, stood before eleven teen-agers. Jostling a stick of chalk in his right hand DiMassa said to them, ''Don't be satisfied with getting a 710 or a 720, but maximize your potential. Don't put pressure on the school. Don't make them find a way to get you in school. You get yourself in school.''

DiMassa was talking to these eleven teen-agers about the Scholastic Aptitude Test. He was telling them what the test consisted of, how to prepare for it, and the minimum score the NCAA accepted in order for them to be eligible to play as a freshman in college.

The reason he was telling them all this was that they would probably be going to college in a year or so, many on basketball scholarships, and DiMassa wanted them to know what to expect.

Throughout Cavanaugh Hall here on the campus of Indiana University-Purdue University in Indianapolis (IUPUI) similar classes were being held, each class holding eleven to twelve students. In all 123 boys were dispersed throughout the building. Not only were they listening to teachers telling them about the SAT, they were listening to lectures in English and math and reading. They were being told what kind of questions to expect on a college application form, what questions to expect from the admissions office during an interview at a college, and how best to present themselves during the interview.

What these 123 teen-agers were attending was the 1991 NIKE Academic Betterment & Career Development camp, known simply as the NIKE camp. Held at Princeton University for the past eight years, the camp was moved to the IUPUI campus in 1991 because of its central location. These young men were considered the best junior and senior high school basketball players in the nation. Four of them were from Indiana. They were 6-foot-11 Brian Gilpin (Mt. Vernon High School, Fortville), 6-foot-7 Charles Macon (Elston High School, Michigan City), 6-foot-9 Walter McCarty (Evansville Bosse), and 5-foot-11 Scott Shepherd (Carmel High School).

The purpose of the week-long camp, say the NIKE officials, is to "simulate conditions for matriculating as a student-athlete at the college level." NIKE hopes that these kids will return to their high schools mindful of the "expectations needed for academic and athletic success in college."

Decked out in Nike T-shirts and gym shorts, and wearing new unscarred NIKE high-top shoes, these kids attend classes each morning from 9:00 A.M. till noon. Counseling sessions are held from 1:00 to 2:00 in the afternoon and from 7:00 to 8:00 in the evening. NIKE emphasizes that basketball plays a minor role at this camp. Indeed, a camper can expect to play only a half hour in the afternoon and another half hour in the evening.

The campers are provided with a workbook that has chapters entitled, "Lecture Note Taking," "Memory Improvement," "Exam Preparation," "Writing College Research Papers," and "Filling Out an Application." In DiMassa's class he holds up a book entitled *Up Your Score,* a book designed to help one improve one's entrance exam scores.

"If you could travel through time and interview a historical figure who would you interview?" asks Mr. Durkin. He looks out over the faces of the twelve campers seated before him. "This is an actual question from a college," he says. "I'm not just making it up. These questions I'm asking you are ones actually asked by admissions officials from Wake Forest, Princeton, and William & Mary. They are asked of people seeking admission to those schools. So, who would you interview?"

At first the campers are all silent, looking down at their desk or sneaking glances at one another to see who will go first.

"Columbus," says one camper.

"Martin Luther King," says another.

"Malcolm X."

"Yea, Malcom X."

"Adolf Hitler," says another, and everybody laughs.

"Thurgood Marshall."

"John Kennedy."

"Malcolm."

"Now also be prepared to say *why* you would want to interview these people," says Durkin. "That's probably the most important point of asking you the question." The campers nod their heads.

Over in another classroom a teacher is asking her students to read aloud.

"But before we begin," says the teacher, "I don't want anyone laughing if someone mispronounces a word. We're here to learn, ok?"

The teacher asks a camper to read aloud. He begins reading from the section in the workbook entitled, "Reading in College." Halfway through the first paragraph the teacher stops the camper. He looks up at the teacher.

"Now, tell me what you just read," she asks him. "No, no. Don't look down at the book," she says, stopping the camper as he starts to look back down at the book. "Look at me and just tell me what you read."

Silence.

The teacher quickly asks the question to the other campers. "What did he just read?" she asks, looking out over her class. Someone answers.

"That's right," she says, "Good. When you're reading, don't just look at the words. Digest them. Pay attention to what you're reading. In college no one is going to be there to hold your hand. You'll be on your own. You've got to be able to function on your own.''

Noon finally rolls around, and the campers file out of Cavanaugh Hall. They cross Michigan Street and enter the University Place Hotel & Conference Center where the campers are housed and fed. They have an hour for lunch. At one o'clock they will be herded into the auditorium to hear the first of four guest speakers scheduled to talk to the campers over the next week. Today's speaker is Dick Vitale.

The floor of the auditorium is littered with wire and cable from the local television stations and from ESPN. Writers from *Sports Illustrated* as well as regional newspapers line the back row. Vitale is good copy. ESPN is recording Vitale's speech and will broadcast it in the fall.

A few minutes before one o'clock the 123 campers stroll into the auditorium. They fill up the front half of the auditorium. At exactly one o'clock Vitale walks through the doors in the back of the auditorium. It is a very warm day in Indianapolis, and he is wearing a T-shirt and shorts, white socks, and tennis shoes (Nike?). As he makes his way down the aisle he shakes hands with the kids, slaps some high fives, pats some backs saying, ''How ya doin'?'' ''Good to see ya.'' When he gets to the bottom of the aisle at the foot of the stage he whips around and hollers, ''Where's Jason Kidd? Where's Kidd?'' (Kidd is from St. Joseph High School in Alameda, California). Kidd stands up and Vitale says, ''Jason! I've been spreading the word about you all over the country. Don't let me down, Jason!'' Vitale steps up to the stage and is introduced. The campers are told that Vitale is not being paid for this appearance.

Vitale doesn't stay on the stage, but comes back down so he can be close to the kids. He speaks for an hour. Well, *speak* is not really the right word. Vitale cajoles, screams, and pleads. Never is his voice less than a roar. He waves his arms, he jabs his finger, he pounds the stage· with the palm of his hand, he grabs kids by the shoulder, he literally thrusts his face within inches of others. His eyes dart across the room. He stalks up and down the aisles; never is he motionless. If you think he is animated on television, you should see him here.

His message? Stay off drugs, have other options other than basketball, take pride in yourself. Mostly, though, his message is to stay away from drugs. And he doesn't start off slow and work his way to a fever pitch. Vitale hits the floor running and immediately kicks into a fast break.

"The big C [crack, cocaine] will bury you!" he roars into the face of a camper. "The only way to beat the big C is not to start. I guarantee you, I swear to you, it will kill you. That's a fact."

He climbs up the incline of the aisle jabbing his finger into the faces of those he passes. He definitely has their attention.

"Look at Len Bias. Oh, Lenny was beautiful. Great body, great moves. The next Michael Jordan. But where is he? History, baby. History! Because of the big C! You can't beat it! Don't play that game!

"And don't tell me everybody's doing it. That's bullshit! That's a loser's attitude! I say screw peer pressure! You have to have strength, and you have to have character.

"I beg you, don't mess with it. Follow the David Robinsons of the world. Look at him. Navy. Character. Diploma. Smarts. He's got it all! Follow him, not Len Bias!

"Oh, you can try to con yourself. You can rationalize. But every morning, you know what? You gotta look in that mirror, and the mirror doesn't lie. You can con mamma, you can con that woman who brought you into this world and lie to her, you can con pappa, but you can't con that mirror! That's real, and it won't go away!

"Fill your mind with knowledge, not drugs! There's no substitute for knowledge! Find things you love to read. Be more than a jump shooter! Don't let the ball use you, you use the ball! Just like David Robinson!

"And be proud. You know what David Robinson and Michael Jordan and Magic Johnson all have in common? Pride! Pride is an ingredient all successful people have! Be too proud for the big C!"

He nearly runs over to a camper who is sitting next to the wall. "I see guys walking around. They're shuffling along, acting cool, not looking you in the eye. That's not pride! That's a cover up! Throw your chest out! Look a man in the eye when he speaks to you! Do the very best you can in whatever you do!"

"I used to teach sixth grade. And I told myself I was gonna be the best damn sixth grade teacher there was. Many of you out there, I know you have dreams. Have them! That's great! But my friend, my math tells me there's only room for a small group of men in the NBA. And think of the millions of kids wanting in! Don't place it all on basketball! Have options! And whatever you do be the best damn one there is!'' Sure, have fun. But why just settle to be a pro player? Why not a player in the game of life? And why just a player? Be the best!''

And on and on it went for an hour. When he finished he was nearly hoarse, and his shirt was sweated through. He received a standing ovation.

18

Things to Come

This story began in Gary, Indiana, at the corner of Harrison and Twenty-fifth Avenue in the Bo Mallard Gymnasium on October 15, 1990—the first day of practice. An explanation of why this was done will yield a little insight into the nature of Indiana high school basketball.

At least half of the fun and excitement, some would say more than half, is the air of anticipation that surrounds the start of the season or the start of the tournament. For the fans of a team that is loaded with talent, to make it to the Final Four is like Christmas. Everyone in town is a little nicer to one another. There doesn't seem to be any awkward moments when people meet, any grappling for things to say. There is always something to talk about, something that is nearly ever present on the minds of the entire town. And that is the upcoming season.

In bars and barbershops, in the elevators and washrooms of office buildings, and anywhere else casual conversation is made, discussions of the upcoming season can be overheard.

"If we can get out of the sectional we're in the Final Four," begins a typical conversation.

"You might be right as long as the coach doesn't play half the team out of position as he did in 1987," comes the retort. "You don't think South will give us any trouble in the regional?"

"No way. They haven't got anybody up front, and our guards are quicker this year, too."

"Yeah, but that Rattermann kid scares me, he has unbelievable range and you know he can score 40 on any given night."

"Yeah, but how is he gonna get a shot off if we put Kavanaugh on him? Kavanaugh might be worthless on offense, but he can play D, and he's grown two inches over the summer so he's taller and quicker than Rattermann now."

Basketball is often said to be a year round sport in Indiana. It is, just as it is in neighboring Illinois and Kentucky. But unlike Illinois, Indiana fans don't have the Sox or the Cubs or the Bears to discuss during the long hot summers. True, the NFL Colts are down in Indianapolis, but not too many folks in Huntingburg are all that concerned about them. The good burghers of Huntingburg are more likely to fret over that blasted full court press of Jasper. And unlike Kentucky, Indiana is not fixated on one institution. In Kentucky, all sports, including high school basketball, take a back seat to University of Kentucky basketball. Oh, the diehard Cardinal fans in and around Louisville might take exception to that, but basketball fans in Hazard or Madisonville pull down Cawood Ledford, the voice of the Kentucky Wildcats, when they flip on that radio, not . . . say, who *does* give the play-by-play for the University of Louisville, anyway?

Conversations like the one given above were taking place in many towns around the state back in June and July. In places like Anderson and Jeffersonville where dominant teams are likely to emerge, it is a safe bet that fans will scan this book to see if a preview of the 1991–92 season is included before they decide whether or not to buy it.

While fans of Terre Haute South, Whitko, and, of course, Gary Roosevelt long to savor the season past, the fans of Anderson, Anderson Highland, and Jeffersonville simply can't wait for October 15, 1991. On that day practice begins, and on that day begins, they hope, *their* season.

Of course, this was the hope of the Martinsville and Evansville Bosse fans on October 15, 1990. It would do no good to remind the Jeffersonville or Anderson fans of this fact. Not getting excited about the upcoming season would deny them half of their fun.

Anderson Highland will likely occupy the number one spot in the preseason poll. Cross town rival Anderson will probably not be far behind. Highland is the kind of team everyone likes in the preseason, because they are a team that "has the whole package." Highland also has a star player capable of carrying the team through the inevitable rough times, too. The star player, Randy Zachary, will only be a junior, and at only 5-foot-10 he is the kind of player that everyone underestimates. That is until they actually see him play.

With his quickness and tenacity, Zachary is often described as a water bug on the court—he seems to be everywhere at once. Add to this his uncanny shooting from three-point range and you have a player very comparable to Travis Ford now playing for the University of Kentucky.

But if anyone still doubts him because of his size, do not doubt his team, the Scotts. Anchoring in the middle will be 6-foot-10 senior and all-state candidate David Foskuhl. Foskuhl made excellent progress offensively in 1990, and he has always been an intimidating defensive player. In the Lafayette Semistate he had an impressive game against Glenn Robinson, and he appears ready to assert himself as a dominant player. With yet another returning starter in guard Brad Ash the Scotts appear, as of October 15, 1991, anyway, to be the team to beat.

Fans in the Anderson area will have the pleasure for two more years of watching the match-up between Zachary and Anderson Indian guard Maurice "Kojak" Fuller. Fuller plus the fact that the Anderson Indians are, well, the Anderson Indians are reason enough for this team to be ranked in the preseason poll. The only team that may be better than Anderson Highland is the Jeffersonville Red Devils, but because they are largely unknown to central Indiana it is likely the Red Devils will not garner enough votes to start the season at number one. Jeffersonville may have been the deepest team in the state last season, and that includes Richmond, and Jeffersonville is returning most of that depth this year.

Junior guard Sheron Wilkerson and sophomore center/forward Corey Norman may be the best of the bunch. Still underclassmen, these two guarantee Jeffersonville a bright future. Joining them will be a pair of 6-foot-3 senior forwards, Joe Estes and Mike Harris. All four averaged well into double figures in the 1990-91 season.

Jeffersonville's rival, New Albany, may also have one of its better teams in years. Junior Noy Castilo may be behind only Zachary and Fuller. In the middle will be 6-foot-8 Pino Pipes once referred to by Glenn Robinson as "one of the most physical players I've ever played against." As good as the Bulldogs will be it is difficult to see them getting by Jeffersonville in the regional.

Expect the North Central Conference to rebound this year. Sending only two teams to the final sixteen and no one to the Final Four is almost unheard of for the state's strongest conference. It is difficult, though, to tell which team other than the Anderson Indians will emerge from the regionals.

As for the marquee seniors—Charles "Killer" Macon, Walter McCarty, Scott Shepherd, and Brian Gilpin—they all seem to be lacking a supporting cast needed to make it to the show. Shepherd will probably have the best chance, and Macon will have the best potential to carry his team to the State Finals. But if it is any consolation to these guys, that is what everybody said about Alan Henderson, too.

And what about the defending champs? Robinson gone, Floyd gone, Harding gone, Woods gone, Graham gone.

Roosevelt gone.

Look for the East Chicago Cardinals, behind 6-foot-5 Maurice Billups and 6-foot-5 Marlon Anderson to come out of the Region, although Andrean might give the Cardinals a scare.

A thunderstorm greeted the morning of September 3, 1991. The needed rain was a little too late, though, to save the corn and beans that had baked in the parched fields throughout the summer. Much of the corn crop was simply being written off.

Be honest, now. If someone would have told you back on October 15, 1990, that in nine months time Communism would die in the Soviet Union, that the Union of Soviet Socialist Republics would disintegrate, that a free-market economy would rise up there, and that the Baltics would be free independent nations, would you have laughed and jeered and labeled as a fool anyone who would have suggested such a thing?

In the world of sports September 3, 1991, found Jimmy Connors nursing some aches and pains. On the day before, Labor Day, the thirty-nine-year-old Connors advanced to the quarterfinals of the U.S. Open at the National Tennis Center in New York by surviving a four hour, forty-one minute slugfest. The ordeal went five sets.

Also on Labor Day, Bo "I Play Two Sports" Jackson returned to the lineup. The baseball lineup. Out the entire baseball season due to a severe hip injury sustained playing professional football, Jackson went 0 for 3 dressed in the pinstripes of the Chicago White Sox.

Florida State was the number one college football team in the country, and Atlanta was just a half a game behind Los Angeles in the National League West.

Down at Kouts High School Marty Gaff, basketball coach and history teacher, stood at the door of the school looking out at the rain. "Where's it been all summer?" he asked of the rain.

He stepped back into the school. Classes were about to end for the day, and over the intercom announcements were being read. He walked over to the empty cafeteria and sat down. "Well," he said, "we had the two week basketball camp here this summer, and we took them down to St. Joseph's College (in Rensselaer) for awhile, I took some time off, and now here I am again. The summer just flew by."

And with the new season drawing closer, Gaff is beginning to think about who is coming back and who he has lost. The biggest loss may be Sam Obermeyer who averaged 22.4 ppg as well as pulling down an average of 11.4 boards per game.

"Larson's at Purdue running track," said Gaff. "He's a good high jumper, you know. Brad [Redelman] is at Kalamazoo hoping to play ball, and Sam is at Bethel [in Mishawaka] playing ball. But we've got some seniors who will step up to help us. Alex Heinold [5–11] and Tom McNeil [6–5] played a lot for us last year, and I think we have some other seniors who can do the job.

"But I don't see us and LaCrosse dominating the conference as we did last year," Gaff continued. "There'll be much more parity this coming year, so I expect a tougher time of it this year. But another thing to consider is the new sectional alignments. This year every sectional will have six teams. Hanover Central and Rensselaer leave the KV [Kankakee] sectional. That means the draw will be even more crucial than before. Also, the KV winner will go to the Michigan City regional. I like that. I think people around here can identify more with Michigan City than Lafayette."

So it might be a struggle to equal or better the 1990-91 overall record of 17-6 and 6-2 conference record. Will the town of Kouts stand for anything less?

"This is a community that is extremely proud of its school," said Gaff who was raised in Noble County, just north of Fort Wayne. "Now, I'm not gonna sit here and tell you that if the team went without a win and continued to lose year after year the town would be pleased. But this community loves this school and backs it no matter what. There was some talk recently of consolidating Kouts with another school. The community would not even hear of it.

"This is a small school. We don't have a football team. We have cross country and volleyball. And basketball. The community just rallies behind its team, its school. And I don't just mean basketball, but the other sports and the academic achievements of the students as well."

But if the opportunity to coach at a larger school would present itself, a school with a larger pool of potential players and with greater resources and facilities to offer, would he jump?

"I deal with great kids here," Gaff said, "both on the court and in my history class. This is a great community, a good place to raise a family. I like it here. Sure, I think about the bigger schools now and then, but I can honestly say I like it here."

But being from the northeastern corner of the state, next to Ohio and Michigan, he can compare Indiana basketball with that of the neighboring states.

"With what I can see," Gaff said, "the game is really no different, except they have the class ball there. What seems to be different there is that Michigan and Ohio don't seem to have the tradition we have. I don't know why that is, but that's my impression.

"That's one of the reasons I like it here," Gaff went on to say, "the community's close. Kouts is not a powerhouse basketball town, but it has its tradition. And it's not always fun. I'm criticized now and then, and I've never gotten used to that, but a new season's coming around and the community gets excited and so do I. Besides, like I said earlier, with all the summer basketball it hardly seems no time before one season ends and another starts."

He walked out of the cafeteria, and from the hallway he could see outside. The rain had stopped. The black clouds were parting, and sunshine was trying to seep through.

"We open against Oregon-Davis the Friday before Thanksgiving," said the forty-one-year-old Gaff. "At O-D."

A Mr. Tom Eliot, no mean poet and one who had what could be called a passing interest in history, once wrote, "In my end is my beginning."

Only forty-two days before the opening of practice.

Endgame

Basketball as it is played in Indiana is no different from anyplace else. Slap plain jerseys on a high school team from Indiana, transport them to Minot, North Dakota, and nobody would know without being told that the players hailed from Hoosierland.

No, what makes Indiana high school basketball different are the fans. For some reason they like the game. A lot. They like the game so much they build extravagant gyms to play it in, pass season tickets onto generation after generation through wills, play state championships that draw 41,000 fans, write books about it. *Why* do they like it so much? Who knows.

During the state finals—in the convention center adjacent to the Hoosier Dome and connected to the Dome by a concourse—another large group of people was gathering. This was the National Conference on the Teaching of Foreign Languages. A couple of reporters covering the state finals wandered into this conference by mistake. Upon seeing the press passes hanging from the shirts of these two reporters, someone from the conference asked them if they were covering the foreign language convention.

"The state finals," the reporters answered, a bit smugly perhaps, amazed that someone would even think that a conference on foreign languages was newsworthy.

"Oh, is there a basketball game here today?"
He was probably from North Dakota, anyway.